Out of the Closet
and
Into the Classroom

Laurel A Clyde
Marjorie Lobban

Out of the Closet
and
Into the Classroom

Homosexuality in books for young people

Out of the Closet and Into the Classroom
Homosexuality in books for young people

First edition
Published 1992 by ALIA Thorpe
a joint imprint of

D W Thorpe
(a part of Reed Reference Publishing)
18 Salmon St
Port Melbourne, Victoria 3207
Australia

and

ALIA Press
(the publishing division of the Australian Library & Information Association)
9-11 Napier Close
Deakin, ACT 2600
Australia

© Laurel A Clyde and Marjorie Lobban

Cataloguing in publication data

Lobban, Marjorie.
    Out of the closet & into the classroom: homosexuality in books for young people.

    Includes index.
    ISBN 1 875589 02 3.

    1. Homosexuality in literature - Bibliography. 2. English fiction - 20th century -
    Bibliography. 3. Gays - Fiction - Bibliography. I. Clyde, Laurel A. (Laurel Anne). II. Title.

    016.8230080353

ISBN 1 875589 02 3

Designed and typeset in 12pt Goudy by D W Thorpe
Cover design: Richard Seakins
Printed in Australia by Impact Printing, Brunswick

Contents

Introduction

There is no more striking evidence of changes in our social attitudes over the last 40 years than that provided by books for young people. Young people's books are regarded (whether accurately or not) as powerful in the formation of attitudes, values and ways of understanding the world. Argument is perennial about the role these books should play in the socialisation of children and young adults. Should children's literature mirror reality, so the world of fiction is recognisable to the reader and therefore credible and able to be identified with? Alternatively, should young people's literature provide an optimisitic word-view, in which traditional values are shown to be effective in ensuring happiness?

Children's literature, especially young adult literature, increasingly explores the uncertainties and unhappiness that many children experience as they grow, and the realities and choices they must face if they are to become mature, independent adults. There are few sacred cows that do not appear in books for young people: rape, incest, death, drug abuse, domestic violence, abortion, teenage prostitution, alcoholism, nuclear devastation and betrayal of trust are all to be found in contemporary writing for children or young adults.

Many young people will recognise by or during adolescence that they are homosexual; others will be confronted by the fact that one of their parents, siblings or friends is homosexual. The recognition of that fact in novels or stories for young people is the main area this bibliography sets out to explore. A secondary concern is to record the social attitudes towards homosexuality that are evident through this literature.

This bibliography deals with homosexuality in books for children and young adults – a topic that simply would not have been discussed with minors in public until quite recently. It says much for the extent of recent changes that six of the books we have listed are picture books for young children, while some others are written to appeal to children in the upper classes of the primary school. Altogether, some 120 books are listed, almost all of them published in the last 20 years.

There has been some argument that a bibliography such as this, no matter how disinterested its compilers may have been, puts a powerful tool in the hands of those who would wish to censor and sanitise what young people read. In other words, that it could be used as a negative selection tool, enabling people to avoid or even dispose of titles that are included here. Such use of the list would be an anathema to us; the aim of the project is to enlighten rather than restrict. The project started as a way of trying to gain some insights into books for young people which may give some insights into the genre. It also promised to highlight changes in prevailing attitudes in society towards young people, homosexuality and what one should know of the other. We also believe that all young people should, at times, be able to recognise themselves or parts of their experience in their literature. This is no argument for unrelieved gritty realism, but a plea for a plurality in young people's books to reflect their own infinite variety of interests and needs.

Scope of the Bibliography
All books included in the bibliography have been published in English – no attempt has been made to cover the books for children and young adults in French, German, and other European languages, though many relevant titles in those languages are known to exist. Only books written for young people, or books which have been cited in standard bibliographies as works for the young, are included. Books for adults about homosexual behaviour amongst young people are omitted, as are books of pornography, whether written for young people or adults. A second list could almost be compiled of books read for this list and rejected – titles such as Edmund White's *A Boy's Own Story*, George Whitmore's *Nebraska*, *Shy* by Kevin Killian, *Miss X or the Wolf Woman* by Christine Crow, *Stealing Time* by Nicky Edwards – all of which have adolescent protagonists but which we judge to be adult books in intention. This judgement is based partly on our own reading and partly on the fact that these books have been published and reviewed as adult or general works, rather than as works for young people. This does not mean that certain adolescent readers would not read and enjoy them, but it does place them outside the limits of this listing.

Two previous bibliographies of adult works on this theme, by Ian Young on male homosexuality and by Barbara Grier on lesbianism, have included titles in which homosexual behaviour or attachments could be inferred – books presenting 'implied' homosexuality or 'latent, repressed' homosexuality, or 'characters who could be so interpreted'. This resulted in the listing in those bibliographies of many works in which we could find no real evidence of homosexuality or discussions of homosexuality. Second guessing authors' intentions or putting their characters under a neo-Freudian microscope is a tricky task at best. We have therefore included only books in which clearly identifiable homosexual characters or incidents are found (whether related to major or minor characters), or in which charges of homosexuality are made, or in which the consequences of a homosexual relationship are dealt with, or in which homosexuality is discussed, or which have been listed in previous bibliographies as fitting into one of these categories. Sometimes the characters or incidents are quite minor, but they usually have a bearing on the plot. This means that we have left out such titles as Barbara Bolton's picture book, *Jandy Malone and the Nine O'Clock Tiger* (Angus and Robertson, Sydney, 1980), in which it is made clear that Jandy and her single-parent mum live with mum's lady friend, but there is no evidence or mention of a lesbian relationship. Similarly, in *Lots of Mommies* by Jane Severance (Lollipop Power, Chapel Hill, North Carolina 1983), Emily lives with her mother Jill in a household with three other women. Whilst this is clearly a feminist household, there is no indication in the text that it is a lesbian one, despite the fact that the book has appeared in previous relevant bibliographies. We have also left out the plethora of early 20th-century British girls' school stories, which may be thought to have some place in this listing, such as Angela Brazil's *Loyal to the School* (Blackie, London,

1920), in which the heroine is even called Lesbia, and A *Patriotic Schoolgirl* (Blackie, London, 1918). A contemporary reading of many of them finds sexual innuendo where none was intended originally. Despite the passionate friendships and the episodes of bed-sharing, suggestions of homosexuality on the part of the authors or the girls would have been well outside the general experience of the time, even though Freud's theories were then gaining some currency in academic circles. Further, the relationships portrayed show the acceptance by society, at the time, of very close relationships between women, with no suggestion of moral boundaries being overstepped.

An illuminating article on these books is 'You're a dyke, Angela', by Rosemary Auchmuty, in the Spring 1987 issue of *Trouble and Strife*. As Gillian Freeman says in her biography of Angela Brazil (1976, p19), 'there are ... friendships between the girls (and sometimes between teachers and girls) with passions, jealousies and misunderstandings, demands of loyalty and honesty, and kisses and embraces which today would be interpreted both sexually and psychologically', but the evidence in the biography indicates that such a retrospective interpretation would be inappropriate. This is not to say that homosexuality was not practised in British boarding schools early this century; just that it is outside the range of these books. Similarly, it would be a fallacy to read homosexual insinuations into early 20th-century boys' adventure titles like *Queer Mr Quern* by the Rev. A.N. Malan (a novel about an insane schoolmaster, published in serial form in *The Boy's Own Paper* in 1902), or even later boy's titles like *Grim and Gay* by Gunby Hadath (an English boarding school story of the second world war period), although to modern ears they would seem to have these implications.

Most of the works listed are fiction, with one or two excursions into literary autobiography. We have not tried to cover factual books or sex education resources aimed at young people, even though a considerable number of these have now been published in which homosexuality is presented either as a lifestyle option or as a valid experience for young people. This does not necessarily mean that these works are designed expressly to promote homosexual behaviour.

While most of the books in the bibliography have been read by at least one of us, there are some titles which were listed in the standard reference works or which were identified in reviews as being relevant to our theme, but which we have been unable to obtain. In each case, these have been listed in our bibliography but our annotation indicates that we have not sighted the title. However, books which we have not sighted are not included in the appendices or in the discussion which follows in this introduction. There are books mentioned in other bibliographies for which we have not been able to locate any information at all, including *School Spirit* by Tom Hale. They have not been included in our bibliography, though they may well be relevant.

Historical Background
Given the traditionally conservative attitudes towards children's reading in the United Kingdom, the United States, and Australia, it is not surprising to find that adult books in English dealing with homosexuality or with homosexual characters predate similar books for young people by many years.

In the last three decades of the 19th century, adult books dealing with sexual variance both increased in number and became more freely available. This was due in part to new 'scientific' theories common at the time which supported the notion that homosexuality was inborn or the result of hereditary factors. Supporting these theories, writers like Richard von Krafft-Ebing, Albert Moll, and Havelock Ellis campaigned for official leniency and general tolerance. While the trial of Oscar Wilde in 1895 for homosexual practices temporarily curtailed the publishing of overtly homosexual books, other factors were at work which led ultimately to increased literary freedom in this respect. One of these was the women's movement, particularly before 1900, which widened women's educational and occupational opportunities and brought about a general relaxation of sexual standards, a trend which accelerated during the world war of 1914-18. Another was the work of Sigmund Freud and his followers in the development of psychology, and Eugene Steinach and Serge Voronoff in the development of endocrinology, which paved the way for more open discussion of sexual matters, at least in educated circles.

With the relative freedom of the 1920s, the number of quality books available dealing with lesbianism or male homosexuality increased. Marcel Proust's *A la Recherche du Temps Perdue* (published in French in 1923, in English as *Remembrance of Things Past* in 1924), Thomas Mann's *Death in Venice*, Virginia Woolf's *Mrs Dalloway* (1925), and Elizabeth Bowen's *The Hotel* (1928), are examples. In London in November 1928, Radclyffe Hall was prosecuted for her novel *The Well of Loneliness* on the grounds of obscenity, specifically because of its explicit defence of a lesbian. As with the Oscar Wilde case 33 years earlier, this had a temporarily restrictive effect, but ultimately the case served mainly to draw attention not just to this work but to others on related themes, and to arouse public curiosity.

After the Second World War, several factors worked towards an increase in book publishing in this field and towards increasing frankness about homosexuality in the books that were published. One was the changes in public attitude and morality brought about by the social disruption of the Great Depression and the war of 1939-45. Another was the publicity that was focussed on homosexuality as a result of Alfred Kinsey's published studies of sexual behaviour in the human male (1948) and in the human female (1953). Together these studies revealed the hitherto unsuspected extent of homosexual behaviour in the community and showed the wide gap between official morality and private sexual activity. The 1960s and 1970s saw the growth of the gay liberation movements, and so writers in this field received more public attention. Through the development of gay magazines and specialist presses, gay writing could be more easily and readily published, though there were still some difficulties in getting gay fiction published, distributed and reviewed. However, the generally more open attitudes of the last three decades have enabled the publication of more novels dealing with male homosexuality or lesbianism by mainstream publishers as well as the gay press, and some of these, like Jane Rule's *The Desert of the Heart* (Secker and Warburg, London, 1964) and Alice Walker's *The Colour Purple* (Harcourt Brace Jovanovich, New York, 1982), have been made into successful films for the general public. Some books originally published by gay or feminist presses have since been republished by mainstream publishers for a wider audience; an example is Rita Mae Brown's 1973 novel *Rubyfruit Jungle*, first published by Daughters Press and now available in Corgi.

Against this background of the gradual relaxing of attitudes towards the portrayal of homosexual characters and the description of homosexual relationships in adult literature, can be viewed a similar development in literature for young people from the late 1960s. Apart from the early books, *Tom Brown's School-Days* by Thomas Hughes (1857) and *The Lass of the Silver Sword* by Mary Constance Dubois (1910), and *The Diary of Anne Frank* (1947) which cannot be categorised with the other books because of its autobiographical nature and because it was not written as a young adult book, there are only two titles on this list of books for young people which predate the 1970s. These are *The Chinese Garden* by Rosemary Manning (1962) and *I'll Get There. It Better Be Worth the Trip* by John Donovan (1969). However, as the annotation points out, the former is probably not truly an adolescent book. Otherwise the books span the years 1970 to 1988 and reflect the flowering of the comparatively recent genre of adolescent literature, including the teenage 'problem novel', as well as the more open approach to homosexuality in adult books.

Appendices VII and VIII make it very clear that the number of books for young people dealing with homosexuality has increased greatly since the early seventies. The 1980s seems in retrospect to be the decade when limitations on content largely disappeared, especially in young adult writing. From 1986 to 1988, 35 books appeared, in comparison to the 30 identified from 1962 until 1979. It has become increasingly difficult to identify titles suitable for this bibliography, as homosexuality is no longer an issue which is so unusual in literature that reviewers feel obliged to mention it. Even in books which would seem unlikely to be relevant to the bibliography (historical fantasy, for instance), it has become more common to find homosexual minor characters, discussions of homosexuality, or the use of homosexual terms. While some evidence of homophobia does remain in books for young people, this bibliography charts a growing acceptance of homosexuality as a natural part of the world, and one which has a legitimate, even necessary, place in literature.

The Books in the Bibliography

A number of books in the bibliography, especially the earlier titles, can be regarded as 'problem novels', whether the 'problem' is homosexuality or something else. Others could be classified chiefly as presenting positive role models, a small number as adolescent romances, while others present homosexuality in an incidental, usually non-problematical way. There has been an increasing number of positive role model books, as opposed to problem novels. The latter certainly do, however, still exist.

Adolescence is a time of growing sexual awareness. It is also a time when individuals try to see their place in the world and become sharply aware of relationships, both their own and those of other people. Hence it is not surprising that most of the books we have identified are adolescent novels. There are however a small number of titles aimed at the pre-pubescent child, such as *Jenny Lives with Eric and Martin, Heather Has Two Mommies*, and *Families: A coloring book*. Books for younger children often interpret their world, and, considering the size of the homosexual population, it is perhaps surprising that references to homosexuality do not occur more frequently and naturally in books which expand and explain the child's world. Those books which are available for young children are mainly the products of specialist gay presses and their intended audience seems to be the children of lesbian and gay parents. In addition, with the exception of the first-mentioned title (*Jenny Lives with Eric and*

Martin) these books for young children have appeared only in the period from 1990 onwards. Gains may have been made in honesty in adolescent fiction, but there is obviously still a long way to go in breaching the barriers of what younger children are thought to be in need of protection from in their books, despite the recent appearance of some titles aimed at the young child.

In reflecting on the chronology, it is clear there has been a marked increase in numbers of titles (over twice as many in the 1980s as the 1970s). Considering homosexual main and supporting characters only, there has also been an increase in the ratio of male to female characters. This increase represents, we think, the higher political profile of male homosexuals and their more aggressive approach to actively trying to change attitudes within the community towards homosexuality. Just as the female experience has lagged behind that of the male as a topic in mainstream literature, perhaps the female homosexual experience will take some years to catch up in books for young people.

There has been no particular increase in the description of sex. It remains, with a couple of notable exceptions, fairly restrained. This is quite in line with heterosexual sex in adolescent books, that is, it is acknowledged as happening much more frequently than it used to be but on the whole is not described in much greater detail than previously. One of the most graphic books on the list, *The Milkman's on His Way*, is 10 years old; *Happy Endings Are All Alike* appeared 14 years ago. *The Boys on the Rock* is eight years old. Jenny Pausacker's *What Are Ya?* (1987) is distinctive in many ways – it is Australian, about females, and quite frank in its descriptions of both homosexual and heterosexual sex. It is also one of the books which offers positive role models to young women rather than being a problem novel.

One of the observations which has been made about homosexuals in young people's books is that they have suffered a high mortality rate. This has led to the view that homosexuality has been accompanied by retribution, and there is some historical evidence for this perspective. However, proportionally fewer characters are being terminated when the increasing number of titles is considered, although the inevitably high mortality rate of AIDS sufferers complicates this generalisation. Justin dies in *The Man without a Face* (1972), Phil is killed in *Trying Hard To Hear You* (1974). In *Dance on My Grave* (1982) Barry meets a violent end, as does the schoolteacher, Hillyard, in *McKenzie's Boots* (1987). Evan is killed off in *The Boys on the Rock* (1984), Max is dying in *A House Like a Lotus* (1984), and in *Night Kites* (1986) Pete's death does not occur during the course of the novel, but the reader has a strong sense of its inevitability. In *Cody* (1987), the narrator Trotsky escapes unscathed but a gay friend is killed in a car crash, and Trotsky's younger brother and his best friend (who is also Trotsky's lover) both die in a house fire. Further analysis needs to be undertaken to determine if their deaths could be interpreted as punishment for their homosexuality or, indeed, if the numbers of deaths is disproportionate to the number that would be encountered in any random sample of adolescent titles.

The attitudes of authors to homosexuality reflect a noticeable movement away from homosexuality as a problem to be faced to a view of it as a valid, albeit sometimes difficult, choice of sexual orientation. Nor do they necessarily now portray it as a stage that will go away, as was the case in early titles such as *The Man without a Face* (1972) or *I'll Get There. It Better be Worth the Trip* (1969). Carolyn Logan's 1988 fantasy novel, *The Huaco of the Golden God*, reflects another change. The homosexual rape scene in this book is presented, without any 20th-century social comment, as a reality of life in the more violent world of the ancient Inca.

There are now more books for young people written by writers who are gay themselves and their attitudes are bound to be different from those of straight writers who choose this subject. Books by writers such as these do not deny the difficulties young people will face when they accept their homosexuality but they also present the possibility of a happy, fulfilling future. Straight writers, whilst appearing to intend to give the same message, often cannot get beyond the trauma. Incidental characters fare much better in this regard. Writers who include gay characters incidentally or as background characters seem to be those who have ideologically 'correct' attitudes towards these characters, for example, Frank Willmott, Nadia Wheatley, Doris Heffron.

It is hard to see books on the list which are romances as being equivalent to those available in their hundreds for heterosexual teenagers. We don't wonder which boy/girl will win the heart of our hero/heroine, whether they'll phone, what they'll talk about, whether they'll put the hard word on. Rees and Pausacker are perhaps the closest, or a title like *Act Well Your Part* (1986), but the homosexuality still remains an issue. *Cody* is a book in which the homosexuality is *not* an issue and relationships are complex and varied, but it is more a novel of adolescent self-discovery.

Can generalisations be made based on the gender of the characters portrayed? There is more explicit gay sex than lesbian sex. David Rees does a lot to create this imbalance, but titles like *The Boys on the Rock, Who Lies Inside, Act Well Your Part* also reflect it. The major difference is that there are more males than females portrayed (65:33), despite the fact that 38 of the books have male authors and 77 have female. Only one male writer has written about a female homosexual character (Bruce Brooks in *Midnight Hour Encores*) but there are 34 instances where female authors have depicted significant male homosexual characters.

Classification of the Books

Barbara Grier, in *The Lesbian in Literature: A bibliography*, uses a four-point classification scheme for titles she lists. This scheme has also been adopted, with the necessary change in focus, by Ian Young in *The Male Homosexual in Literature: A bibliography*. Her categories are:

- major lesbian character and/or action/event in the story;
- minor character and/or event;
- implied or inferred lesbianism, 'latent, repressed lesbianism or characters who can be so interpreted';
- 'trash', pornography, books of poor quality, regardless of the quality of the portrayal of lesbian characters or action.

We have elected to omit the final two categories from our bibliography, the third because of difficulties in identification, the fourth because most bibliographies also omit this group and it is probably less relevant to books for young readers. Most of the works we have listed therefore fall within the first two categories. However, we felt that these two categories were inadequate for our purposes, in that they did not provide enough differentiation, and so we have adopted the following four-point schema:

- main character and/or event in the story homosexual;
- supporting character or characters homosexual;

- background character or characters homosexual;
- mentions of homosexuality or the use of homosexual terms (usually as an insult).

Appendices I-IV provide lists of books which fall into each of these categories.

In books in the first category, the main character (usually a teenager) is homosexual, has homosexual tendencies, or discovers that he/she is homosexual. In some of these, coming to terms with one's own homosexuality, or learning to accept one's homosexuality, or developing an identity and lifestyle as a homosexual is the major theme, and the main focus of the book. In Nancy Garden's *Annie on My Mind*, Liza has to accept that she is a lesbian before she is able to see her relationship with Annie in true perspective; in *In the Tent* by David Rees, Tim fights his own 'civil war' in his mind before he can accept his homosexuality and establish a satisfactory relationship with Ray. In some of the books, the homosexual incident, while involving the main character, is comparatively slight, though it is usually very important in terms of the plot. In John Donovan's *I'll Get There. It Better Be Worth the Trip*, the two boys are caught asleep together on the living room floor after they have raided the alcohol supply and then, slightly drunk, indulged in some mild petting. The hysterical reaction of Davy's mother has a profound effect on both boys. In *Hey, Dollface*, by Deborah Hautzig, two girls, also misfits and lonely at their private school, as the boys were in John Donovan's book, share a bed one night when one of them 'sleeps over'. Again, it is the overblown reaction of a parent that awakens them to an awareness of homosexuality and its implications, and causes them to think about the nature of friendship and love.

In books in the second category, the homosexual character is a supporting character, or there is a homosexual incident which involves a supporting character. In each case, this has an influence on the main character and on the plot of the book. In the picture book *Jenny Lives with Eric and Martin* by Susanne Bosche, for instance, five-year-old Jenny lives with her father, Eric, and his lover, Martin. Her lifestyle reflects this alternative family background, and the prejudice she encounters relates directly to it. In Norma Klein's teenage novel *Breaking Up* Alison, the central character, is forced to make choices when, after her parents' divorce, her mother moves to New York and sets up in an apartment with Peggy, her lover. In neither case is the arrangement shown as having long-term adverse effects on the children concerned. In *Night Kites* by M. E. Kerr, it is the brother of the main character who is homosexual; when Pete is diagnosed as having AIDS, Erick, his parents, and his friends all have to make adjustments in their thinking and their attitudes, and it is these adjustments that provide the focus for the story.

The third category relates to those books in which a background character is homosexual, or where a homosexual incident involves a background character. Again, this usually has some influence on the development of the plot, or is significant for the development of one of the main or supporting characters. Books which fall into this category include M. E. Kerr's *Is That You, Miss Blue?*, in which the relationship of two lesbian teachers is used as background in order to demonstrate the values of the church school, where a lesbian relationship is tolerated while a teacher who talks to Jesus is sacked; June Jordan's *His Own Where*, in which lesbian relationships reflect the character of a girls' home; and *Go Ask Alice*, in which the revelation of a homosexual relationship between two boys forces Alice to recognise what her drug addiction is doing to her.

In books in the fourth category, there are isolated mentions of homosexuality, or use of homosexual terms (usually as an insult). This probably reflects a generally greater public awareness of homosexuality which is demonstrated in casual speech and attitudes. We found it interesting that, increasingly, even in books in which there are no homosexual characters or events, homosexuality is discussed freely by various characters, along with a wide range of other topics. It is clear that homosexuality, as a topic of teen or sub-teen conversation, has 'come out of the closet'. Examples of such books include Eileen Fairweather's *French Letters*, in which friends Jean and Maxine speculate on an accusation that they are 'lezzies'; and Barthe DeClements' *I Never Asked You To Understand Me*, in which the father of one of the girls accuses them of being lesbians because they spend a lot of time together, and the girls discuss this. Disturbingly, we found an increased acceptance of the casual use of homosexual terms as terms of abuse: terms like 'faggot', 'lezzie', 'poof', 'dyke' are frequently used as insults in situations often unrelated to their real meaning. This is the case in some books in this bibliography. For instance, in Sandra Chick's *Push Me, Pull Me*, teenage Cathy hears her mother's boyfriend accuse her mother of being a lesbian when she is too tired for sex after a day at work; while in Louise Fitzhugh's *Nobody's Family Is Going To Change*, terms like 'faggot' and 'flit' are applied to seven-year-old Willie when he is determined to be a dancer. In books like Frank Willmott's *Suffer Dogs* and Barthe DeClements' *I Never Asked You To Understand Me*, the terms are quite crudely applied, though in ways that are appropriate for the characters concerned.

Conclusion
This bibliography charts a period of great change in the depiction

of homosexuality in children's books. From near invisibility or the isolated, daring and unhappy depiction of a tortured central character in a story, we have moved to a situation where homosexual children and adults now often appear as secondary or background characters, as well as central characters, part of the fabric of the novel rather than its focus. Where the main character in the novel is homosexual, this is likely to be shown as something that that character has to accept about himself or herself, whilst that character is also discovering that his or her sexual orientation can encompass a happy, loving and fulfilled life. Since 1986 there has been an enormous growth in the number of titles which fall within the parameters established for this list. In addition, it has become increasingly difficult to identify potential titles, both because of their quantity and because reviewers and publishers' blurbs often no longer specifically mention homosexual characters and incidents. We feel that the books listed represent a discernible growth and change in the way sexual preference and sexuality is presented to young people in their literature. It is interesting that this change has occurred over a relatively short time span – only a little more than 20 years.

Out of the Closet
and
Into the Classroom

ANONYMOUS

Go Ask Alice
Corgi, London (1971)
ISBN 0-552-09332-7

Go Ask Alice purports to be based on the diary of a 15-year-old drug user, who, after attempting to kick her habit, dies of an overdose. The homosexual incident in this book is slight, but it does influence the plot. Alice and her friend, Chris, sell drugs to little elementary school children to help their boyfriends, Richie and Ted, through college. As Alice says, 'since I'm Richie's chick all the way, I have to do what I can to help him'. When they walk into the boys' apartment one afternoon and find Richie and Ted in bed together, they are so shattered that they make an attempt to go straight. Alice, furious at herself for being sufficiently gullible to be drawn into supporting 'a couple of queers', turns them in to the police for pushing drugs to young children, before running away with Chris to make a new start in California.

BARGAR, Gary

What Happened to Mr Forster?

Clarion Books, New York (1981)
ISBN 0-395-31021-0

K ansas City in the 1950s is the setting for this gentle, rather sad novel. Louis enters sixth grade determined not to be the class baby any longer and to establish himself as a real person with his classmates. Help comes from an unexpected quarter in the person of the new sixth-grade teacher, Mr Forster. He patiently coaches Louis in baseball, brings out his talent for writing and engages the whole class in a project to stage a play which Louis writes based on the Arthurian legends. Mr Forster is entirely circumspect with his students, but when it is discovered by some parents that he is living in a homosexual relationship in a nearby town, community pressure forces the school to sack him. Louis is devastated by the loss of Mr Forster, but also at the unfairness of his dismissal, and he is one of the few people to speak out in Mr Forster's warm defence. He is also terrified of once again becoming the class wimp, but in one last meeting with Mr Forster he is inspired to continue being the new independent Louis, even without his teacher's presence. The novel has an air of innocence through the naive voice of the narrator, and Louis's reaction to Mr Forster's dismissal marks his rite of passage into independent adolescence.

BENNETT, Jay

Masks
Watts, New York (1971)
ISBN 0-531-01979-9

This title is listed by Barbara Grier in *The Lesbian in Literature* (third edition, 1981) as a work for young adults in which lesbian incidents or characters have a part. It is described in the second edition of *The Lesbian in Literature* (p 13) as 'a juvenile novel, intended for ages 12-14. It is clearly, though in a fairly minor way, lesbian in emphasis, with a stock ending. A milestone ...'
A copy of this book has not been sighted.

BESS, Clayton

Big Man and the Burn-Out

Houghton Mifflin, Boston (1985)
ISBN 0-395-36173-7

A bandoned by his unmarried mother who could not tolerate farm life, Jess lives with his grandparents in rural Oklahoma. *Big Man and the Burn-Out* deals with Jess's uneasy relationship with his prickly grandmother, and with the development of his friendship with Meechum, a boy whose behaviour problems have caused him to repeatedly fail at his junior high school. Jess and Meechum are helped by a sympathetic teacher, Mr Goodban, who lives with a male friend, Vic, and whose school nickname is 'Gay Goodban'. However, while some reviewers have made much of 'this book with a homosexual teacher in it', Mr Goodban's sexuality is not discussed and it is not an issue in the book. Rather, it is simply a fact there in the background: some teachers are heterosexual, others are not, and that is the way the world is. In an article in the February 1988 issue of *Voya*, Clayton Bess commented that the problem appeared to be not so much that there was a homosexual teacher in the book, but that Mr Goodban was presented as an effective, caring teacher rather than as a 'tormented and twisted individual' or 'a child molester'.

BLOCK, Francesca Lia

Weetzie Bat
Collins, London (1990)
ISBN 0-00-673630-0

This book was first published in the United States in 1989. Weetzie Bat, the teenage daughter of a divorced mother, lives in Los Angeles. She becomes good friends with Dirk, a boy at her school; Dirk is gay, and has a boyfriend called Duck. Dirk's grandmother gives Weetzie a magic lamp, whose resident genie grants her the traditional wishes. Weetzie, of course, wishes for a boyfriend. When Grandmother dies, Dirk, Duck, Weetzie and Weetzie's wished-for boyfriend, known as My Secret Agent Lover Man, move into grandmother's house. Weetzie wants a baby, but My Secret Agent Lover Man is too scared and takes off, so Weetzie gets into bed with Dirk and Duck (so no-one will know who the father is). The result is baby Cherokee. My Secret Agent Lover Man returns and gets involved with strange events apparently relating to voodoo; there is some involvement with witchcraft; a baby is dumped on the doorstep and nicknamed Witch Baby; Weetzie's father suicides; Duck decamps in a fit of depression but is subsequently found by Dirk. And finally Weetzie, My Secret Agent Lover Man, Dirk, Duck, Cherokee, Witch Baby and assorted animals, live happily ever after in the same house. All this happens in 88 pages, to the accompaniment of some vaguely enunciated New Age philosophy.

BOSCHE, Susanne

Jenny Lives with Eric and Martin

Gay Men's Press, London (1983)
ISBN 0-907040-22-5

J enny is five years old, and she lives in Denmark with Eric and Martin. Martin is her father, and Eric is his lover. This picture book for young children shows the daily life of this 'family', through black-and-white photographs, line drawings, and simple text. As would be expected from this publisher, the book presents the case for the acceptance of homosexual lifestyles. When a woman on the street screams 'You gays! Why don't you stay at home so the rest of us don't have to see you?' to Eric and Martin, for instance, and Jenny is upset, Eric draws a picture story for her to show her that 'it can never be wrong to live with someone you are fond of'.

BRANFIELD, John

Brown Cow
Gollancz, New York (1983)
ISBN 0-575-03223-5

Girls are objects of curiosity and distant lust to Andy until he becomes acquainted with the delectable Gloria when he is 17. Set in Yorkshire just after World War II, the book follows Andy's halting progress with Gloria and his growing responsibility at school where he is unexpectedly made head boy. There he attracts the attention and assistance of a master nicknamed 'Bummer' Carrington who is entirely circumspect and encourages Andy to study for entrance to Cambridge. He also introduces him to Duncan, a journalist of even more dubious reputation, who undertakes Andy's education in the arts. Gloria finally accuses him of being homosexual and Andy realises he has outgrown her. He has had no advances made toward him by either man; he is conscious of how much he values their friendship and company but also sure he is heterosexual. Branfield's is a subtle novel, capturing both the period and Andy's awakening to the adult world with a sure touch.

BRANFIELD, John

Thin Ice
Gollancz, London (1983)
ISBN 0-575-03350-9

I n this sequel to *Brown Cow*, the head boy Andy Trewin skates on thin ice in his friendship with Duncan, a young journalist who takes evening classes in literature. Duncan confesses his homosexuality and introduces Andy to his homosexual friends. In 1947 homosexuality was a punishable offence, and Andy is made aware of this when police question him about Duncan. The latter is given an 18-month jail sentence, which shocks Andy into reassessing his life.

BROOKS, Bruce

Midnight Hour Encores
Harper and Row, New York (1986)
ISBN 0-06-020709-4

When Sib tells her father she wants to meet her mother for the first time, she has no idea how frightened he is, that he may lose her or that she will be terribly disillusioned by the meeting. As they drive across America to her mother's home, Taxi tells her about her mother and tries to help her understand why she had abandoned Taxi and Sib as a baby, 16 years earlier. He plays the music of the era and tries to recreate for Sib the hedonistic hippie days into which she was born. They call in on an old friend of Taxi's, a stunningly beautiful woman who is now living with a tough-looking female lover. Gwen, too, has a child that she has chosen not to keep because, she says, she thought being a lesbian would have gone against her in a custody battle. However, Sib feels that her motives were much more selfish. Gwen and Dolores form part of the pattern of past times and people against which Taxi tries to put events into perspective for Sib. They are superficial and stock characters, portrayed rather unsympathetically.

BUNN, Scott

Just Hold On
Delacorte Press, New York (1982)
ISBN 0-440-04257-7

Stephen is a quiet, reserved boy, isolated by his father's alcoholism from the seemingly carefree lives of his peers. Charlotte is similarly alienated from her adolescent classmates by the tortured memory of an incestuous incident between her and her father which left her psychologically scarred and vulnerable. They each recognise the pain in the other without ever revealing themselves fully, and become friends and then lovers and their relationship is their passport to acceptance as part of the gang. Stephen is further troubled by his attraction to the popular and attractive Rolf, and the signals he seems to get from Rolf despite his macho bravado. On a French excursion to New York everything comes unstuck – Charlotte breaks down, Stephen and Rolf finally sleep together, Stephen's father dies – and adolescent trauma is unbounded. The end of the novel is more concerned with Stephen's reconciliation with his father's memory and Charlotte than his acceptance of his sexuality. A final summmary of characters and what happened to them makes no reference to it, although Stephen is at peace with himself, unlike the permanently damaged Charlotte. A fairly depressing novel with a message of qualified survival.

CHAMBERS, Aidan

Dance on My Grave
The Bodley Head, London (1982)
ISBN 0-370-30366-0

S ixteen-year-old Hal faces charges of wilful damage when he is caught dancing on his friend Barry Gorman's grave shortly after the funeral. The reasons for Hal's extraordinary behaviour emerge through a report he writes for the social worker assigned to his case, at the suggestion of a sympathetic teacher. In a brief seven weeks, Hal meets up with the hedonistic but attractive Barry, and they form a homosexual relationship. It soon becomes clear, however, that while Hal feels deeply about Barry, to Barry the affair represents just another in a long string of conquests. When Barry sleeps with a young girl they have both met, Hal's jealousy causes an argument, and Barry storms out. His death, in a motor cycle crash only hours later, leaves Hal feeling guilty and profoundly depressed. The characterisation in this tightly constructed novel is excellent, and the homosexual relationship, while obviously intense, is treated with subtlety and sensitivity.

CHICK, Sandra

Push Me, Pull Me
The Women's Press, London (1987)
ISBN 0-7043-4901-9

Fourteen-year-old Cathy is raped by her mother's crass new live-in boyfriend, Bob. Unable to talk about the incident because she fears no-one will believe her, Cathy has to cope alone with the pain and the guilt. Her mother, preoccupied with her disintegrating relationship with Bob, has little time for Cathy. She starts to rebel at school, and even alienates her best friend Sophie until, very slowly, she begins to work out her anger. Two brief incidents in the book are relevant, in different ways, to the theme of this bibliography. In one gym changing-room scene with Sophie, Cathy realises that she is attracted to her – but this feeling is based as much on a need for security in a relationship as it is on physical attraction. In the other incident, Cathy hears Bob use the word 'lesbian' as a term of abuse when her mother is too tired for sex with him – and this leads her to reflect on Bob's working-class prejudices.

COLEMAN, Hila

Happily Ever After
Scholastic, New York (1986)
ISBN 0-590-33551-0

Melanie has loved Paul since she was a little girl, when he befriended her at school. As they grow to adolescence, they become an accepted pair around school and enjoy the mutual delight of their approving parents. Yet some part of Paul has always been inaccessible to Melanie and she has developed a repertoire of excuses to explain his off-handedness, his lack of passion towards her, his restlessness and reluctance to make plans for the future. When they are 16, Paul finally confesses to Melanie that he is gay and she feels as if her whole world has fallen apart. However, since their long-standing friendship is still important to her, she supports Paul strongly after she succeeds in persuading him to come out with his family. When the book ends, Paul is sure of himself and happy, and his family is becoming reconciled. This is an interesting variation on the teenage romance, and one which is handled with considerable sensitivity and restraint.

DeCLEMENTS, Barthe

I Never Asked You To Understand Me
Viking Kestrel, New York (1986)
ISBN 0-670-80768-0

S tacy and Dianna are two teenage girls who attend an alternative high school for problem students. As their disintegrating family life pushes them closer to desperation, they rely on their friendship to keep going. Because they spend so much time at each other's houses, Stacey's uncouth father accuses them of being lesbians: 'You girls got something going together?' For both of them, this comes as a shock. Despite the brevity of this scene, the book is included in the bibliography as an example of a recent work in which accusations of homosexuality are freely, though erroneously, made, and the topic is discussed.

dePaola, Tomie

Bonjour Mr Satie

Ashton Scholastic, Gosford (1991)
ISBN 0-86896-645-2

Mr Satie and his friend Fortie travel the world together. On a visit to Paris Mr Satie and Fortie are at the salon of Gertrude and her companion Alice ('our dear American friends living in Paris'), when a showdown develops bewteen artists Pablo and Henri. Mr Satie is called upon as a disinterested man of impeccable taste to arbitrate on the relative artistic merits of cubist Pablo and post-impressionist Henri. This is a highly sophisticated picture book, lusciously illustrated by the author. Much knowledge is assumed in the reader: Gertrude's walls are covered with famous paintings and there are references to a portrait in blue painted by Pablo of Mr Satie. To an adult reader Mr Satie and Fortie are obviously a gay couple, and their dear Parisian friends are Gertrude Stein and Alice B Toklas. Neither of these things is important however for a reader to enjoy the book; responding to the rich lode of artistic allusion is much more significant.

DONOVAN, John

I'll Get There. It Better Be Worth the Trip

Dell, New York (1969)
ISBN 0-440-93980-1

At the age of 13, Davy goes to live with his alcoholic mother in her New York apartment. Neglected by his mother, lonely, and unhappy at his new private school, he relies on his dog for company until he makes friends with the equally lonely Altschuler. During a game at Davy's apartment, they almost accidentally kiss each other, enjoy it, worry about it, but then decide that 'tough guys' like them 'can't be queer'. One evening, they raid a bottle while Davy's mother is out, get tipsy, and fall asleep together on the living room floor. Her hysterical accusations of 'unnatural behaviour' when she finds them later almost destroy their friendship. At the end of the book, they come to terms with the idea that what they have done isn't really so bad, but decide that once they have 'made out with a few girls' they won't have to think about it. All this is, perhaps, a little pat as a conclusion.

DRESCHER, Joan

Your Family, My Family

Walker, New York (1980)
ISBN 0-8027-6382-9

This 32-page picture book for two- to five-year-olds shows all kinds of families (including adoptive families, foster homes and extended families). Margo and Rita are described as Peggy's family, with the comment that 'although Margo is her real mother, Peggy feels as if she has two mothers'. As in Meredith Tax's book *Families* and Jane Severance's *Lots of Mommies*, there is no explicit statement that the family is a lesbian one, although this has been inferred by reviewers, with some reason.

DUBOIS, Mary Constance

The Lass of the Silver Sword
Century, n.p.(1910?)

J eannette H Foster, in *Sex Variant Women in Literature* (p 255),
lists this as the only known children's book with a lesbian or
variant focus to be published in English early in the 20th
century. It first appeared in serial form in *St Nicholas Magazine* in
1909 and was subsequently published in book form by Century.
Of it, Foster says, 'centered about the adoration of a 14-year-old
girl for a senior of 19 in her boarding school, it was sympathetic
but so circumspect as to lack full vitality'.

It has not proved possible to read a copy of this work.

ECKER, B A

Independence Day
Avon Flare, New York (1983)
ISBN 0-380-82990-8

Mike is 16 and coming to accept the fact that he is homosexual. He finds himself strongly drawn to his oldest and inseparable best friend Todd, but is petrified of Todd's reaction if he dares reveal himself. He finally sets himself a date, Independence Day, when he will tell Todd and begin to come out to the rest of the world. In a fairly long and basically uneventful novel, Mike moves towards Independence Day learning more about himself and what it means to be gay, observing all sorts of relationships, and deciding what he values. He finds that his father's best friend from childhood is gay, is helped by a sympathetic teacher with a gay son, and accepts that the delectable Todd is truly straight. When Mike finally does come out it is to a fairly tolerant and supportive family and friends (Todd had already guessed). While perhaps having a rather rosy resolution, Mike's first person narrative conveys his adolescent pain and turmoil with conviction, emotion and dignity.

ELWIN, Rosamund and
PAULSE, Michele

Asha's Mums
Women's Press, Toronto (1990)
ISBN 0-88961-143-2

This Canadian paperback for young children is illustrated by Dawn Lee. In simple language, it tells the story of Asha, whose class is going on an excursion to the Science Centre. The teacher asks all the children to have a form signed by their parents, giving permission to go on the trip. But when Asha returns her form, signed by her 'two mums', she is told to take it home again and have it filled out correctly. The muddle is sorted out when one of her 'mothers' visits the school and explains matters to the teacher. Meanwhile, Asha has worried about being allowed to go on the trip, and has answered a lot of questions from her classmates about having two mothers. For instance, classmate Coreen says, 'My mum and dad said you can't have two mothers living together. My dad says it's bad.' To which Asha replies, 'It's not bad. My mummies said we're a family because we live together and love each other.' However, beyond this, there are no discussions, or mentions, of lesbianism, in contrast to another major picture book in this bibliography, *Jenny Lives with Eric and Martin*, which is quite explicit about homosexuality, even showing the two men in bed together.

FAIRWEATHER, Eileen

French Letters: The life and loves of Miss Maxine Harrison, Form 4A

The Women's Press, London (1987)
ISBN 0-7043-4903-5

This book has been included in the bibliography as an example of one in which a homosexual term is used as a form of abuse. Jean's brother Bob calls Jean and Maxine 'a pair of lezzies', and teases them about their relationship in a heavy-handed way, simply because they are very close friends. Told chiefly through letters, the story reflects teenage concerns and activities in modern Britain.

FARMER, Penelope

Year King
Atheneum, New York (1977)
ISBN 0-689-50090-4

Eighteen-year-old Dylan, in his first year at an English provincial university, faces a personal identity crisis as he attempts to come to terms with his relationship with his more favoured twin brother. Because he has no girl friends, his mother and his brother suspect him of being 'queer'. However, when he drops out of university and moves to a cottage in rural Somerset, he acquires a job and develops a sexual relationship with Novanna, an American teenager living temporarily on a farm with her aunt. This book was the subject of considerable critical comment when it was first published because of numerous descriptions of various sexual practices, including oral sex. However, even this fails to sustain interest in the story. Apart from Dylan, the characters are one-dimensional (Novanna, for instance, is presented only as a sex object), and mild excursions into the paranormal detract from, rather than add to, the story line. The suspicions voiced about Dylan at the beginning of the book are the only reason for its inclusion in this bibliography.

FITZHUGH, Louise

Nobody's Family Is Going To Change
William Collins, London (1976)
ISBN 0-00-671351-3

Emma and Willie Sheridan are children of a wealthy black American lawyer. Emma, aged 11, earns her chauvinist father's disapproval when she announces that she wants to be 'the best lawyer in the country'; both her parents believe it is a totally unsuitable profession for a woman. Seven-year-old Willie, who longs to be a professional dancer like his uncle Dipsey, also falls foul of his father, who wants him to follow in his path as a lawyer. The struggle of the two children to have their personal goals recognised by their parents forms the basis of this excellent book. It is included in this bibliography because derogatory homosexual terms like 'faggot' and 'flit' are used as insults when Willie maintains his determination to dance. Emma, for instance, calls him a 'faggot' on the first page, a fellow student says 'Get you Mary' when Willie dances in the school corridor, and Dipsey spends some time trying to convince Willie's mother that not all dancers talk in 'high, fluting voices' and 'swish around'.

FOSTER, Aisling

The First Time
Walker, London (1988)
ISBN 0-7445-09835-5

I n this British novel for late teens, one of the secondary characters, Martin, turns out to be gay. Martin works at a take-away chicken place with Rosa, the central character, who is in her last year of school. Quite a few current social issues and ideas are canvassed in this book: Rosa's mother is an activist who frequently goes on protest marches; a friend develops anorexia; Rosa's mother considers abortion when she finds herself unexpectedly pregnant, and subsequently decides to have the baby but to continue life as a single parent. Amongst all this, it is not surprising to find that homosexuality is also introduced.

FOX, John

The Boys on the Rock
Arrow, New York (1985)
ISBN 0-09-938040-4

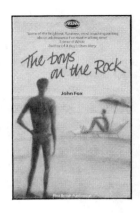

I t's 1968, New York, and Billy is 16. He and his friends hang out, smoke dope, and go on dates with girls from the local Catholic school. Billy finds his dates quite unmoving and the boys on his swim team much more stimulating. He restricts expression of his preference to graphically described self-gratification until he is befriended by the slightly older and more experienced Al, a fellow worker for McCarthy's presidential campaign. Their sexual encounters are quite explicit; their emotional engagement is shallower. Billy seems, for the period and his age, unrealistically at ease with his sexuality and is fortunate to have the beach house of a tolerant aunt in which to pursue the affair. More literary than *The Milkman's on His Way*, the book is nevertheless similarly obsessed with the physical.

FRANCIS, Jaye

Rebecca

(Hot Pursuit Series, 4) Penguin, Sydney (1991)
ISBN 0-14-013425-5

Rebecca is the fourth and last book in a series called 'Hot Pursuit' designed for teenagers. The four interconnected books (*Melissa*, *Franca*, *Louise* and *Rebecca*) follow the lives of a group of students at an Australian high school, although each book has a different heroine and is told from a different point of view. There is some reference to incidents and characters in previous titles, and a continuing mystery is detected throughout the four books. Essentially teen romances, these books nevertheless rise above the limitations of the genre through discussions of current social issues and a more rounded approach to the characters. Rebecca, the heroine of the fourth book and a minor character in the other stories, is presented as being quiet and withdrawn, possibly someone with a problem. In the fourth book we find out what the 'problem' is – Mum is a lesbian. There is some discussion of sexuality in the book, but after questioning her own sexuality, Rebecca ends up firmly in the arms of one of the boys. However, attitudes to lesbians in the book, as to other issues raised, are ideologically very 'correct' and positive.

FRANK, Anne

The Diary of Anne Frank

Pan, London (1954)
ISBN 0-330-10737-2

This well-known diary was written by the young Jewish teenager, Anne Frank, while she and her family were in hiding from the Nazis in a secret annexe of a commercial building in occupied Amsterdam during the Second World War. First published in Dutch in 1947, it was later translated into English and published in London in 1953. Aged 13 when she first went into hiding, Anne was 15 when she died in Bergen-Belsen in 1945. In one short passage in the diary, Anne reflects on the changes in her body, her awareness of her sexuality, and her growing appreciation of herself as a unique person. She describes an incident from earlier times when, in bed with a girl friend, she kissed her and wanted to feel her breasts. She records her disappointment at the girl's refusal, then comments, 'I go into ecstasies everytime I see the naked figure of a woman, such as Venus, for example. It strikes me as so wonderful and exquisite.' There is no other evidence of lesbian feelings in the diary, and this passage should be seen in the context of Anne's exploration of her own mental, emotional, and physical development. She subsequently toyed with the idea that she was in love with 17-year-old Peter Van Daan, whose family was in hiding with hers.

FRICKE, Aaron

Reflections of a Rock Lobster: A story about growingup gay
Alyson, Boston (1981)
ISBN 0-932870-09-0

a story about growing up gay

I n this book, the author describes his experiences of 'growing up gay' in the United States, from early childhood to the final years of high school. The basis for his story is that he did not 'choose homosexuality', rather that homosexuality was a trait with which he was born. Much of the book is devoted to his fight in his senior high school year to be allowed to attend the high school prom with his friend Paul as his date. His experiences of prejudice at school and in the wider community are detailed: physical and verbal abuse in the gym locker room, seeing the word 'gay' painted on the storm door of his parents' house, comments by teachers about 'fruit cocktail' in the classroom. These lead him first to 'come out' and then to make an issue of being treated differently from the heterosexual teenagers in his class. Assisted by the National Gay Task Force, he mounts a successful challenge in the federal court to the school's decision to refuse to allow him to take a male escort to the prom.

FUTCHER, Jane

Crush
Avon, New York (1981)
ISBN 0-380-67462-9

S et in an exclusive American girls' boarding school, this book almost steams with high emotions and suppressed teenage sexuality. Jinx, in her last year of school, develops a crush on a fellow student, the fascinating but wayward Lexie. A night of cuddling in bed one vacation convinces Jinx that she wants a deeper relationship, but Lexie simply takes advantage of her devotion while indulging in a hectic, illicit affair with her cousin Phillip and forming passionate friendships with other girls. The book raises questions about the nature of love, friendship, and loyalty, but at a fairly superficial level. When the relationship between Lexie and Jinx is revealed publicly, the school authorities show a rather prurient concern with the physical aspects but little interest in morals or truth, and it is this which finally shatters any illusions Jinx has left about the school and the way in which people are judged in our society.

GARDEN, Nancy

Annie on My Mind

Farrar, Straus, and Giroux New York (1982)
ISBN 374-40413-5

Liza Winthrop, a freshman at the Massachusetts Institute of Technology, recalls and reflects on the previous year, her last at school, when she met and fell in love with Annie Kenyon. In clear, compelling and often lyrical prose, the story of their affair emerges as Liza attempts to come to terms with all that happened to both of them. While their overwhelming mutual physical attraction is made very clear, it is their emotional involvement that really underpins the book. The depth of characterisation and the beauty of the language used by the author make this one of the most impressive books in the bibliography.

GLEITZMAN, Morris

Two Weeks with the Queen

Pan, Sydney (1990)
(First published by Blackie 1989)
ISBN 0-330-27183-0

Twelve-year-old Colin Mudford already felt a little resentful and jealous of his younger brother Luke, so when Luke collapses suddenly on Christmas Day and becomes the total focus of the family's attention that resentment deepens. Luke has terminal cancer, and Colin is packed off from the Australian bush to stay with relatives in England to protect him from the sadness of Luke's inevitable death. In his daydreams Colin is convinced that somehow he will save Luke, and be hailed a hero by his parents. He appeals to the Queen, tries to contact the best cancer doctor in the world, and finally comes to realise that it is Luke who is most important, and that being with him and loving him is the best thing he can do. He is brought to this realisation by his friendship with Ted, whom he meets in a London hospital where Ted is visiting his lover Griff, dying of AIDS. Colin sees most things in black and white, and when Ted is bashed for being a 'Queen' it doesn't make sense to him: 'All the blokes in the world doing really mean and cruel stuff and getting away without even a smack in the ear and here's a bloke getting bashed up for being in love with another bloke.' He supports both men with his simple unquestioning friendship, and Griff's inevitable death shows him that he wants to be home with Luke when he dies. This is a humorous and compassionate book for quite young readers.

GUY, Rosa

Ruby
Bantam, New York (1979)
ISBN 0-553-12274-6

I n this sequel to *The Friends*, the spotlight shifts from Edith and Phyllisia to Ruby, Phyllisia's quiet, gentle older sister. Ruby at 18 feels alone and lonely; her father and sister seem cut off from her and she feels estranged from her classmates. She pursues a friendship with the magnificent Daphne and is whirled into an all-consuming love affair. The ecstasy of their relationship is powerfully described and when Daphne coolly decides that her life plan can't include Ruby, her despair is equally poignant. Rosa Guy's prose is lyrical and the book is distinguished by emotional honesty and its complex, credible characters.

HALE, Keith

Cody
Alyson, New York (1987)
ISBN 1-55583-105-2

Trotsky, new to Little Rock, Arkansas, soon becomes best friends with the charismatic Cody. Trotsky longs to have a physical relationship with Cody but Cody is straight and it is not until they have been friends for many months that they become lovers. Their friendship is a supportive and intensely intellectual one and that remains more important than its physical dimension. Trotsky also has a young lover called Mark who is his 14-year-old brother's best friend. What distinguishes this book, apart from its lyrical writing, is that his homosexuality is a non-issue for Trotsky – he doesn't agonise over it and is quite accepting of it, as are both his brother and his politically active and aware mother. Love-making with Cody is described in spiritual rather than physical terms, although encounters with Mark are a little more earthy. This is a book where the most important thing about the main character isn't his homosexuality, but his discovery of himself as a person through his relationships with many people.

HALL, Lynn

Sticks and Stones

Dell, New York (1972)
ISBN   0-440-9866-9

Although homosexuality is discussed in this early 1970s novel, and one of the main characters is homosexual, the theme of the book is really the destructive power of vindictive gossip. Tom has moved with his divorced mother to a small town in Iowa, where he is completing his final year of high school. He becomes friendly with Ward, a writer who has been discharged from the Air Force because of a homosexual affair. A boring and uncouth boy, whose somewhat clinging company Tom has rejected, avenges himself by spreading the rumour that Tom is also homosexual. This costs Tom his right to compete as part of the school team at the state music championships, leads to his isolation from his classmates, and almost costs him his friendship with Ward. Despite the fact that Tom and Ward did not have an affair, both suffer as much as if they had. Although the old nursery chant says 'sticks and stones may break my bones, but names can never hurt me', it is scandal-mongering which is shown to be the destructive force here.

HALL, Lynn

The Boy in the Off-White Hat

Charles Scibner's Sons, New York (1984)
ISBN 0-684-18224-6

Thirteen-year-old Skeeter has a summer job at the Okay Corral in Arkansas, looking after the nine-year-old son of Maxine, the owner. Shane proves to be easy to mind, particularly since there are horses to ride and country things to do. However, when businessman Burge Franklin arrives in the little town and begins to pay considerable attention to Maxine and Shane, Skeeter starts to notice ominous changes in Shane's behaviour. Where he had previously enjoyed trips with Burge, he suddenly begins to show fear of him, and appears generally uncomunicative and unhappy. When Maxine invites Burge to move in, Shane runs away – and it subsequently becomes apparent that Burge has been molesting Shane. While the sexual activity itself is not described, the fact that it took place is made clear through its effect on the various characters, and through later discussions with a social worker.

HANLON, Emily

The Wing and the Flame

Bradbury, New York (1981)
ISBN 0-87888-168-9

Fourteen-year-old Chris spends the summer days with his friend Chris, and with Owen, a reclusive 71-year-old sculptor who lives nearby. As the summer progresses a three-way friendship develops, which is explored in the light of the theme of the novel, the complexities of love and friendship. Eric's parents become suspicious of Owen's interest in a young teenager like Eric, but they are finally able to appreciate the positive effects of the relationship. Meanwhile, Eric and Chris are drawn closer together as the summer progresses, and though their attraction is initially detrimental to their friendship, ultimately the friendship is strengthened because of it.

HAUTZIG, Deborah

Hey, Dollface
Fontana, London (1978)
ISBN 0-00-671964-3

oth misfits at their new private school in New York, Val
and Chloe rapidly become close friends. The intensity
of their feelings for each other lead them to think about
the nature of friendship and love. One night, they share
a bed when Val sleeps over at Chloe's place, and friendship turns
to sexual awakening. Feelings of guilt, and fear of being labelled
lesbians, almost destroy their friendship, until they come to terms
with both. The central question in the book, posed by the author
through Val, is 'how do you separate loving as a friend and sexual
love – or do they cross over sometimes?'.

HEFFRON, Dorris

A Nice Fire
and
Some Moonpennies
Macmillan, London (1971)
ISBN 333-12773-0

azie McComber is a 16-year-old Canadian Indian girl who sees life as a series of experiences to be welcomed. This book is about her latest experience – hitch-hiking to Toronto with her dog Doggit for a few days to try some marijuana. Among the people she meets are Sonia and Kit, who provide her with a bed for the night. Her surprise when she discovers Sonia and Kit are lesbians is quite comical, and though the incident plays a very small part in the book, it does cause her to reassess her values.

HELLBERG, Hans-Eric

I Am Maria
Methuen, London (1978)
ISBN 0-416-85110-X

An eccentric book for those used to British, American, and Australian novels, *I am Maria* tells of Swedish Maria, sent to live temporarily with a foster family whose conservative, strict outlook is very much at variance with her previous upbringing. Maria finds solace in the friendship of Pia whose family espouses the philosophy 'you could do anything you liked as long as it didn't hurt anyone else'. A short incident when Maria and Pia have a sauna, shower, put on pyjamas and cuddle together in Pia's bed seems to me the only reason for its inclusion, I think quite inaccurately, in a previous bibliography. Attention is drawn to this incident in a review in the April 1979 issue of *Reading Time* (pp 41-42), but the author of the review, Peg Goode, likewise concludes that there is little cause for the publisher's warning on the dust jacket about the book's 'frankness'. The style is staccato and rather un-English; the story subtle, ironic, rich in observation of society and people.

HERON, Ann and MARAN, Meredith

How Would You Feel if Your Dad Was Gay?

Alyson, Boston (1991)
ISBN 1-55583-188-5

W ritten for children of lesbian and gay families, this book is designed to address their special concerns and problems, through a series of 'real-life situation' pieces. For example, when Jasmine announces in class that her father is gay, her brother is upset, claiming that she had no right to reveal a fact that he wanted kept secret. The publisher's blurb claims that 'this is the first book to provide role models for children in these non-traditional families and to give insight into the unique problems they face'. While presented as a story, the text is quite self-consciously didactic, so that it might even be claimed that this is a manual or guidebook for young people, rather than a book of fiction.

HILTON, Nette

Square Pegs
Collins/A&R, Sydney (1991)
ISBN 0-207-17370-2

quare Pegs has a promising start. Denny, a rather unremarkable 15-year-old boy in a NSW coastal town, takes up dancing in pursuit of the delectable Bethany. Friendship blossoms not only with Bethany but also with Stephen, a charismatic, flamboyant fellow dancer. Denny then becomes the victim of a merciless campaign of bullying at school, where he is obliquely accused of homosexuality because of his friendship with Stephen. Family tensions complicate Denny's life and there seems to be no-one to whom he can turn. The author captures teenage dialogue and concerns unerringly, but Denny's isolation, and the fact that no-one seems aware of the attacks to which he is subjected, is unrealistic. The reader is never clear as to whether or not Stephen is gay; the point being perhaps that it doesn't matter, because whatever he is Denny values his friendship dearly. This does however beg the question which would engage most adolescent readers: if Stephen is gay does that mean Denny is gay for desperately wanting to be his friend? The book contains plenty of perjoratives about gays, balanced only by Stephen's Greek-god perfection, and Stephen is at best an ambiguous role model.

HOLLAND, Isabelle

The Man without a Face
Lippincott, New York (1972)
ISBN 0-397-31211-3

Charles is 14 and totally at odds with his four-times-divorced mother and older and younger sisters, each of whom has a different father from him. An avenue of escape is boarding school and in order to pass the entrance exam Charles seeks coaching over the long summer vacation from a mysterious solitary man, badly disfigured from an unknown accident, who lives alone near his mother's summer house. Justin McLeod, the man without a face, becomes the focus of Charles' life over the summer – he is his intellectual mentor, his best friend, and the father he has never known and, as weeks go by, Charles also feels a strong physical attraction to the man. One night when his beloved cat is killed and there is no one to turn to, Charles goes to Justin's house and spends the night with him and presumably makes love with him. It is the end of their relationship but their love has been a positive, healing force for them both. Justin dies shortly afterwards from a heart attack. He has been an intensely romantic figure in the book and his death seems almost a sacrifice to Charles' future maturity unencumbered by sexual ambiguity.

HOY, Linda

Kiss: File JC 110
Walker, London (1988)
ISBN 0-7445-0826-6

I n this thriller for older teenagers Julian Christopher appears to be under surveillance as an enemy of the state. As a child of trendy, 'yuppie' parents with radical views, he has joined organisiations like the Young Communist League which are regarded as subversive. Disillusioned with the world as he sees it, he tries to find a path through life which is more rewarding and more noble. His diaries, stolen by British intelligence, reveal a sensitive young man's search for meaning. Julian's investigator Jamie, a few years older and already cynical about the sordidness of his profession, is drawn to Julian and a physical relationship develops. At the end of the novel the inevitable betrayal of trust and love leaves Jamie unchanged, but is shattering and destructive for Julian. While this book is unquestionably a thriller, it extends the boundaries of that genre through its treatment of themes such as the nature of human relationships and the search for a purpose in life.

HUGHES, Thomas

Tom Brown's School-Days
Macmillan, London (1857)
[no ISBN]

Hughes attended Rugby School during the great Dr Thomas Arnold's reign as headmaster. This well-known mid-19th-century school story, set in Rugby, is based on his own school days, as his comments in the novel make clear. Although the book has been listed in several bibliographies on homosexuality, including Ian Young's *The Male Homosexual in Literature: A bibliography*, the only justification for this would seem to be the following short passage: 'He was one of the miserable little pretty white-handed, curly-headed boys, petted and pampered by some of the big fellows, who wrote their verses for them, taught them to drink and use bad language and did all they could to spoil them for everything in this world and the next'. To this sentence is appended an author's footnote about this 'small friend' system and the comment, 'I can't strike out the passage; many boys will know why it is left in'.

HULSE, Larry

Just the Right Amount of Wrong
Harper and Row, New York (1982)
ISBN 0-06-022645-5

This book is listed in a bibliography by Christine Jenkins as a novel for young adults with a gay theme; it deals with gay relationships, homophobia, and the destructive power of gossip in a small Kentucky town. A copy of the book has not been sighted.

IRELAND, Timothy

Who Lies Inside
Gay Men's Press, London (1984)
ISBN 0-907040-30-6

Jumbo, 18, and in his final year at his English secondary school, is the ultimate jock – rugby team member, fond of beers at the pub with his mates, and with plans to go to teachers' college to become a physical education teacher. Then he gets to know Richard, a quiet, studious boy in his class, and falls in love with him. At first he fights against his feelings, fearful of the taunts of his friends, who despise 'poofters', and of his father, who is a 'man's man'. But even making love to Margaret one night fails to convince him of his own heterosexuality; in fact, it simply highlights his feelings for Richard. In the final chapter of the novel, Jumbo and Richard, together on the beach, discuss their love, accept it, and decide that words like 'homosexual' and 'heterosexual' label a person in a way that is unacceptable. Life is more complex than those labels would indicate. This book was a winner of the Other Award in 1984.

JONES, Rhodri

Different Friends

(Adlib Paperbacks), Andre Deutsch, London (1987)
ISBN 0-233-98096-2

F our boys, Chris, Shaun, Danny, and Azhar, were good friends at their British primary school, but they begin to grow apart as they grow up and their interests change. Chris (Christakis) reports Shaun's brushes with the law, Danny's increasing involvement in black politics, and Azhar's teenage affair with a young man who owns a cafe. This relationship causes Chris to reassess his own values and to rethink his ideas about love. Chris is very much aware that many people, including his own parents and boys with whom he went to school, are hostile to the idea of gay relationships – comments about 'poofs' make this clear. However, after Azhar tells him about his affair with Jeff, Chris finds that there are also many people around who, while not gay, are nevertheless very accepting of gay people. The basic message of the book is that 'it's their life' and everyone has a right to find happiness in his or her own way.

JORDAN, June

His Own Where
Dell, New York (1971)
ISBN 0-440-93648-9

uddy and Angela, black teenagers in New York City, attempt to create a place and a life for themselves when he is orphaned and she is thrown out of home. Award-winning black poet and author June Jordan recreates beautifully the black language of struggle and love, toughness and tenderness. When Angela is placed in protective custody in a home for girls after being beaten by her father, Buddy searches for 'their own where', a place where they can be together. Meanwhile, in a brief sequence in the story, Angela encounters all the realities of a girls' home, including homosexual relationships among the girls and rumours of lesbian behaviour among the nuns who run the place. There is no description of homosexual behaviour, however, the episodes come up only in conversation and are used to show the character of the home.

KERR, M E

Is That You, Miss Blue?
Dell, New York (1975)
ISBN 0-440-94036-2

As a new student at an exclusive Episcopal boarding school for girls in Virginia, 15-year-old Flanders Brown observes the people around her while she settles into a new world of rules and restrictions. One of her preoccupations is with the strange Miss Blue, who lives in nearby rooms and has, she says, a special relationship with Jesus. However Flanders also watches the relationship of Miss Able and Miss Mitchell, who cast long and loving glances at each other, pass each other notes, and request hymns like 'Thou Hast My Heart' at chapel services. In relation to them she is simply a passive observer who does not speculate beyond what she actually sees. What is apparently a homosexual relationship plays a very small part in this excellent book.

KERR, M E

I'll Love You When You're More Like Me
Harper and Row, New York (1977)
ISBN 0-06-023136-X

Wallace Witherspoon Jnr is heir apparent to his Long Island family's funeral parlour business. Sabra St Armour is a teenage television soap opera star. Harriet Hren uses the traditional 'nasty female' tactics of the romantic novels to establish a relationship with Wally. Wally's gay friend, Charlie Gilhooley, is the town outcast after telling his family and friends that he prefers boys to girls. Wally's parents want him to take over the business even though he wants to go to college, Sabra's mother wants to live through her daughter, while Charlie wants to be accepted by family and peers. By the end of the book, Wally and Sabra have taken steps to separate themselves from the goals of their parents and work towards their own goals. Charlie, on the other hand, chooses to bury himself in the small town, where no gay lifestyle is possible. Thus, as one reviewer has commented, while both straight and gay friendships are described, the future promises a sex life only to the straight (Virginia Wilder, reviewing the book in the third 1978 issue of *Interrracial Books for Children Bulletin*, p 14).

KERR, M E

Night Kites
Harper and Row, London (1986)
ISBN 0-06-023253-6

N ight kites are proudly different – they fly alone and unafraid in the night sky, glowing with tiny lights. In the course of the novel, 17-year-old Erick's comfortable life is changed irrevocably by two night kites – the worldly, outrageous Nicki and Erick's brother Pete. Nicki is Erick's best friend's girl until she pursues and ensnares him in an exclusive, passionate affair. Then Pete, his adored older brother, becomes very ill and is diagnosed as having AIDS and Erick has to accept not only his approaching death but also his hitherto unsuspected homosexuality. Nicki's unceremonious dumping of him when she finds out about Pete forces Erick to look inward as he never has before; his aloneness gives him an empathy with Pete and respect and affection for his convictions and courage. The author writes perceptively of people and relationships, and the emotions and reactions of Pete and his family are honestly and movingly portrayed.

KESSELMAN, Wendy

Flick
Harper and Row, New York (1983)
ISBN 0-06-023182-3

Over the weeks of a summer camp at a riding ranch in Wyoming, Nana discovers her sexuality – first as she falls for wholesome fellow-camper Pete, and then when she has a passionate crush on the beautiful and elusive Flick. Flick is from a fractured family and is desperately seeking love. She is manipulative, exploitative, unfaithful, amoral and to the younger Nana completely captivating. Their relationship develops a strong physical element which both enter into and enjoy wholeheartedly, without question or apparent guilt. Flick is also the lover of the groom on the ranch, and later, while Nana is visiting her house, has sex with a boy in the living room while Nana awaits her. The focus of the book is the charismatic character of Flick, rather that the two girls' sexual orientation. The writing, like the hothouse atmosphere of the girls' school, is rather overblown.

KLEIN, Norma

Taking Sides
Pantheon, New York (1974)
ISBN 0-394-82822-4

I n one of the author's early novels for teenagers, Nell and
Hugo's divorced mother lives with Greta in a large house and
shares a room with her. While some reviewers have assumed
that the mother and Greta are lesbians, this is never stated.
Since the two women are background characters, the children
living mostly with their father, their relationship is not integral to
the story and there is no real reason why it should be explored.

KLEIN, Norma

Breaking Up
Avon, New York (1980)
ISBN 0-330-29293-5

Sixteen-year-old Alison's divorced father is appalled when he discovers that her mother, his former wife, is involved in a lesbian affair. He threatens to go to the courts to keep Alison and her brother Martin with him in California, rather than allowing them to return to their mother in New York to finish high school. Though he tries to get Alison to see his view that 'living in a household with two homosexual women' would not be good for her, she eventually comes to realise that her mother's lifestyle choice is her own business, and that her friend Peggy makes her happy. The author presents a range of views about homosexuality, from revulsion to total acceptance, though the basic message, put in a rather heavy-handed way by a teacher at Alison's school, is that 'people are all different' and we 'should respect individual differences'.

KLEIN, Norma

Family Secrets
Dial, New York (1985)
ISBN 0-8037-0221-3

P
eter and Leslie's families have known each other for years, and they have spent their summers in the same town. Then, the summer Leslie is 16, she and Peter begin a teenage affair. But then Peter's father and Leslie's mother marry, after divorcing their respective spouses, and life changes for everyone. Meanwhile, back at school, Leslie is involved in school drama productions, and one of the girls in the cast, Petra, is gay: 'last year [she] had the school in an uproar because she walked around hand in hand with her girlfriend, Cindy...' Petra also jokes about her homosexuality at play rehearsals. Peter works in a research lab in his final semester of high school and finds that one of the male researchers in the lab is gay. Leslie's feminist studies class discusses what it means to be gay. In other words, comments about homosexuality, discussions of homosexuality, and homosexual secondary characters have a place throughout this teenage novel, although its basic theme is the disruption caused by divorce and remarriage. Mostly, the treatment is matter-of-fact, even uninvolved, as is the treatment of the heterosexual liaisons and marriages which are the basis of the book; it is written very much from the viewpoint of an objective outsider.

KLEIN, Norma

My Life as a Body
Alfred A Knopf, New York (1987)
ISBN 0-394-89051-5

Augustine, a native New Yorker, clever, articulate, but socially awkward, is in her final year at high school. During that year, she becomes acquainted with the physical and sexual side of her being and finds her body is often a treacherous companion. Her closest companion during this year of discovery is her best friend Claudia, who has been aware that she is a lesbian for some time and, by contrast, is very comfortable and happy with her body and her sexuality. Augustine is not gay but she and Claudia share their experiences with their partners and love (or lust) objects, trying to fathom the mysteries of relationships and attractions. Augustine's intense first romance is with Sam, a disabled fellow student, and they are still in love when she goes to college. Here she is sustained by the close friendship of Gordon, who is also gay. The relationship with Sam inevitably ends and she begins an affair with one of her teachers, whose ex-wife has ironically become Claudia's first serious lover. Different ways of love and loving are presented without judgement, although the only descriptions of sex are heterosexual. The content of the novel makes this a fairly sophisticated example of the young adult genre, but its straightforward style also makes it very accessible.

KLEIN, Norma

Now That I Know
Bantam, New York (1988)
ISBN 0-553-05472-4

N ina is 13 and if not exactly happy about her parents'
divorce, at least accepting of it. Their joint custody
of her means she spends the weekdays with her
mother and the weekends with her father. Her
mother is still bitter about the breakdown of her marriage and
men in general so Nina and her best friend Dara plot ways to
introduce her to new, suitable men to counter her unhappiness.
On the whole life with Dad is much easier and much less tense,
until he tells her that his good friend Greg is in fact his lover and
is going to move in. Nina cannot accept either her father's
homosexuality or his decision to have Greg move in without
talking to her about it first. Klein as usual brings a light touch to
what could be a heavy topic, and Nina's reconciliation with her
father is gradual and credible. Sharp observations of her
relationships with her mother, Dara and her first boyfriend
counterpoint Nina's shifting feeling towards her father.

KLEIN, Norma

Learning How To Fall
Bantam, New York (1989)
ISBN 0-553-05808-6

Seventeen-year-old Dustin winds up in a psychiatric hospital because his father Skeet believed it was the only solution to the 'problem' of Dusty's mood swings and his intense involvement with his girlfriend Star. But the person who helps most is Star's best friend Amelia Egan, whose close-knit family seems to offer him a haven. Dusty's parents have been divorced for 12 years and Skeet is a reformed alcoholic. Dusty's lawyer mother Connie is gay, but this is not related to his problems, it is simply part of the background. As he says to a friend, 'My mother's gay, and she's about the only adult I know who has a decent relationship with another adult'. Both he and his friend applaud this evidence of good adjustment: 'Hats off to your mother. Anyone who can live with another human being for more than six months and not want to kill him deserves the Nobel Peace Prize.' Dusty and Amelia visit Connie and her friend Twyla in San Francisco, and the household is presented as a normal, well-organised but relaxed one.

KNUDSON, R R (Rozanne)

You Are The Rain

Delacorte, New York (1974)
ISBN 0-4409-9898-0

Barbara Grier lists this book in her bibliography *The Lesbian in Literature* (third edition, 1981) as a work for young people in which lesbian incidents or characters have a place. While Knudson has written several books dealing with lesbianism or with lesbian characters, this is the only title of hers which Grier identifies as being for a young audience. A copy of this book has not been sighted.

KOERTGE, Ron

The Arizona Kid
Joy Street-Little Brown, Boston (1988)
ISBN 0-316-50101-8

This book is listed in Christine Jenkins bibliography as a book for young adults with gay characters and a background of life in the gay community, in this case in Tuscon.

A copy of the book has not been sighted.

L'ENGLE, Madeline

A House Like a Lotus
Farrar, Straus, Giroux, New York (1984)
ISBN 0-374-33385-8

Sixteen-year-old Polly O'Keefe, a young American abroad, finds herself alone in Athens. Events which have led her there are revealed by flashbacks which form the main part of the novel, interspersed with her present experiences and the ultimate healing of the emotional wounds of the past. During the previous summer Polly had become the protege of wealthy, autocratic Maximiliana Horne who has, unbeknownst to Polly, returned to the home of her childhood to die. Local gossip makes Polly aware that Max and her longtime companion Ursula are lovers but she continues the relationship, which Max sees as a replacement for the daughter she lost in infancy. One night Max, drunk and fearful of her approaching death, makes advances to Polly who flees, shattered, and refuses to have contact with her. Her acceptance of Max's truly disinterested love and her forgiveness of Max mark her acceptance of different sorts of love and is a rite of passage to maturity.

LEONARD, Alison

Tinker's Career
Walker Books, London (1988)
ISBN 0-7445-0812-6

Tina is 15, lives with her father and stepmother, and knows nothing of her real mother save her name and that she is dead. Suddenly, Tina wants to know more about her mother and why everything about her has been wiped so completely from her life. She travels to London, following a small clue which leads her to her mother's sister Louise, and the truth. She finds that her mother and grandmother died from Huntington's Chorea and that there is a 50% chance that both she and Louise will develop the disease as they reach middle age. Tina has led a sheltered life and it is not only the disease and her mother's suicide that she has to accommodate as she stays with her aunt. Louise is a lesbian, living with Diana, and their best friends are Red and Jess, a gay couple. They are free-thinking and open in a way totally alien to Tina, who finds the horizons of her world expanding at a dizzying rate. There is a slight implication that Louise lives with Diana because she is too frightened of passing the disease on to children to have a heterosexual relationship; this is rather ambiguously denied by Louise. This curious novel pursues many issues, some on a fairly adult level, in what is clearly a story of a girl's self-discovery intended for mid-adolescents.

LEVY, Elizabeth

Come out Smiling

Delacorte, New York (1981)
ISBN 0-440-01378-X

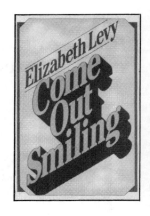

Fourteen-year-old Jenny's stay at Camp Sacajawea, a girls' summer camp in upstate New York, is marred by the discovery that her favourite counsellor Peggy is a lesbian. Her ambivalent feelings about this are heightened by the cracks of some of the senior girls, and by her own father's comments about 'dykes' when he visits the camp. Since she still has a crush on Peggy and enjoys her company, she is confused, at first wondering if she herself is 'queer', then speculating about what it is that Peggy and her girlfriend do together, then wishing the whole subject of sex 'would just go away'. The ending doesn't present an easy solution for the reader, but we are left with the impression that Jenny will achieve what she wants. While obviously written for teenagers, the book has a plain, unattractive cover that would be more suited to an adult non-fiction book.

LIMB, Sue

Big Trouble Orchard
(n.p.) (1990)
ISBN 1-85213-262-0

J ane is a teenager living with her single mother, and the many emotional difficulties she faces, particularly in respect of members of the opposite sex, are the focus of this book. Her mother's new boyfriend Tony moves in with them, and while Jane doesn't mind this since she likes Tony and his teenage son, she soon encounters unexpected problems, such as when Tony makes sexual advances to her. Tony's son Andy is going out with Jane's best friend, though he later discovers he is attracted to Jane. Meanwhile, Jane is interested in both the young men who have moved in next door, who turn out to be a homosexual couple. There are other problems and even crises, too – Jane indulges in a bad bout of drunkeness, her grandmother has a stroke and Jane goes off to care for her, and her mother and Tony separate. The minor homosexual characters in this book are part of a very varied and rather cluttered cast, and the events concerning them are only a small part of the fabric of a wide-ranging story.

LOGAN, Carolyn F

The Huaco of the Golden God
Angus and Robertson, Sydney (1988)
ISBN 0-207-15730-8

Western Australian writer Carolyn Logan taught in Peru for some time, and this novel for young people is based on her experiences of Peruvian life and culture. In a valley near his home, young Huascar digs up an ancient huaco, a puma figurine with special powers. After this, he finds himself drawn into the mind and body of a boy from the ancient Inca past, a boy who is likewise called Huascar. When the modern Huascar sets out on a journey to get medical help for his sick sister, he is also plunged across time into the dangerous quest of his earlier counterpart. One incident, an important one in terms of the development of the plot, makes this book relevant to the theme of the bibliography. While travelling on foot, the first Huascar is badly beaten up by one of the runners who sped up and down the Inca road with messages. Then, as he shelters in a roadside hut to recover, he is raped by two other messengers. The homosexual rape incident itself is described with sensitivity and restraint, but the trauma suffered by Huascar as a result is made very clear. In terms of the social realities of the ancient Inca world as we know them, and as they are presented in the book, the incident is believable and its incorporation in the story is appropriate.

MACFARLANE, Aiden and
McPHERSON, Ann

Me and My Mates
Pan, London (1991)
ISBN 0-330-31615-X

A most curious presentation of facts, fallacies and general information about AIDS. It follows a group of British students through two days around an end-of-school social, with succeeding chapters written from the viewpoint of different people in the group. There is wholesale drunkeness, attempted debauchery and drug using, with, as a connecting thread, the different individuals' reflections on AIDS – their knowledge of it, their fears and the changes it has brought about in the way they live their lives. Naturally, there is some discussion of homosexuality. One of their teachers has recently been absent from school a lot and there are rumours he is gay and suffering from AIDS. At the end of the book he is reported as dying from the disease. A variety of viewpoints is canvassed and there is no moral high ground taken. Information from AIDS pamphlets is reproduced verbatim and the emphasis is on young people making their own informed, thoughtful decisions. As a piece of fiction it wears its heart too obviously on its sleeve.

MACLEAN, John

Mac
Pan Horizons, London (1987)
ISBN 0-330-30489-5

Fourteen-year-old Mac, sent for a physical examination, is indecently assaulted by the male doctor. Mac is completely ill-equipped to deal with the feelings of confusion and guilt that follow; his turbulent emotions, a developing inferiority complex, a fear of homosexuality, contribute to a change in his personality and in his relationships with others. He alienates his friends, argues with his parents, and fails at school. Finally, a woman counsellor at his school breaks through the barriers of secrecy and fear behind which Mac has hidden. The first person narrative means that the reader is totally involved with Mac and his problems.

McCAULEY, Carole Spearin

The Honesty Tree
Frog in the Well, Palo Alto, California (1985)
ISBN 0-9603628-6-X

This book has appeared on several booksellers' lists of novels for young people, probably because the narrator/hero, Tinker, is 12 years old when the major events in the story take place. However, a reading of the book makes it clear that it is an adult novel with a young central character – in the style of Harper Lee's *To Kill a Mockingbird*. When Tinker, who does odd jobs at a plant nursery in her small American town, accidentally reveals that her employers are lesbians, the full force of local prejudice and outrage is directed against the women and their business is almost destroyed. All this is seen through the eyes of Tinker, who tries to make sense of the views and feelings that are revealed. While anti-gay sentiments are presented and discussed, and the problems of a homosexual lifestyle are made clear, the book is far from anti-gay in its treatment.

MALONE, John (compiler)

First Loves
Collins, Melbourne (1989)
ISBN 0-7322-73-8-0

This collection of 15 short stories includes the work of Elizabeth Mansuitt, Rosemary Donovan, Margaret Pearce, Richard Goodwin, Christine Chudley, and Alan Close. All the stories deal in some way with the subject of first love, but the treatment and mood of the stories varies enormously. One of the stories, Alan Close's 'Outside Collarenabri', relates to the subject of this bibliography. It focuses on a family's discovery that a son is homosexual.

MANNING, Rosemary

The Chinese Garden
Jonathon Cape, London (1962)
ISBN 0-946189-70-6

Alison Hennegan, in her introduction to the 1984
edition of this book, describes it as an adult novel of
school life rather than a novel for young people, and
while it is listed in some bibliographies as a young
adult work, Hennegan's judgement appears to be accurate. The
theme is that of innocence corrupted by knowledge and
experience; the writing is sensitive and at times poetic. Rachel
Curgenven, a 16-year-old pupil at Bampfield, a strict British girls'
boarding school in the 1920s, learns about the awakening and
betrayal of love when she is unwittingly drawn into a school
scandal. Her friend Margaret is found naked in bed with another
girl, and Rachel is required to prove that she was not involved in
a 'nameless and abominable act' that she does not really
understand. The crime of which the two girls are accused is
comprehended by Rachel only in retrospect, but in the meantime
her belief in truth and justice is destroyed.

MARSDEN, John

The Journey
Pan, Sydney(1988)
ISBN 0-330-27171-7

The Journey is set in a world very like our own, but also very different. One of its traditions is that a young person, in order to be considered an adult, must go on an extended personal journey and return with seven stories to tell. The book describes the journey of Argus, who is a young man of 14 when he leaves the farm of his parents on foot. He returns a couple of years later with a young woman whom he plans to marry.

The Journey was mentioned more than once to the compilers of this bibliography, however we have been able to find only one oblique reference to justify inclusion, and that reference is intended as a joke. On a wet night, when he is sheltering temporarily in a stable with a stallion, Argus strips to dry himself on a horseblanket, and remarks to the nervous stallion, 'Don't worry ... I won't be bending over in front of you'.

Apart from this, what appears to have troubled people is that there is a minor character in the book who is apparently a hermaphrodite; he/she works in a travelling fair as a half man-half woman exhibit. Although Argus is understandably curious about him/her, there is no evidence that the curiosity is sexual; there is also no evidence that the man/woman has any sexual interest in the hero (or others connected with the fair), although there is a comment that he/she entertains the curious of the towns in his/her caravan after hours for profit. But the problem of deciding which, if any, of the relationships of a hermaphrodite are homosexual is one which the compilers would prefer not to have to solve. The author's point in introducing such characters as the half man-half woman and the two-headed lady is to show that all people are 'freaks', in the sense that they are unique while sharing many of the same human experiences and emotions.

MEYER, Carolyn

Elliott and Win
Atheneum, New York (1986)
ISBN 0-689-50368-7

Neither Win nor his best friend Paul lives with his father. They become part of an organisation called Amigos which brings together such boys and men who will spend time with them and be father figures. Paul's is just a regular guy, but Win gets Elliott, a wealthy cultured man who introduces him to a whole new world of food, and the arts. Paul's immediate reaction is that Elliott must be a 'fag', and Win had better watch out. Win comes to value Elliott's friendship greatly and is not particularly concerned with his sexuality. When Win's first girlfriend is savagely raped in front of him, Elliott is the only person who can give comfort and reassurance, and by the end of the novel Elliott's sexual orientation, never revealed, is shown to be quite irrelevant to their relationship. Win and Elliott move fairly unrealistically to their closeness considering the very different worlds they come from. Paul receives a swift and shattering retribution for his intolerance when he goes to stay with his natural father for the first time and finds him living with a male lover. The author covers a lot of issues in this book, with the persistent theme being that friendship and acceptance are the most important things in life.

MIKLOWITZ, Gloria D

Goodbye Tomorrow
Delacorte, New York (1987)
ISBN 0-00-672913-4

A lex, an American heterosexual teenager, is diagnosed
as having ARC (an AIDS-Related Complex) more
than a year after having a blood transfusion. He has
some of the symptons of AIDS, is a carrier of the
virus and knows that many people with his condition advance to
AIDS. The book centres around his family's and his friends'
fearful and guilty reactions to the news of his illness.
Homosexuality is mentioned only in the context of discussions
about the ways in which AIDS is transmitted. There are no
homosexual characters in the book and, apart from a light joke,
there is no suggestion that Alex might be gay.

MOSCA, Frank

All-American Boys
Alyson, Boston (1983)
ISBN 0-932870-44-9

Neil and Paul, both 17-year-old American high school boys, meet when Paul's family moves to a new neighbourhood. It is love at first sight for the two boys, and their affair begins in the first week they know each other. This causes problems with both their families and with some of the boys at school. Paul is badly beaten up and almost killed by a group of youths who are 'queer bashing', while Neil's racing pigeons are found dead with the word 'faggot' written across the wall in their blood. Neil is attacked later by the same group; he is able to use his kung-fu training to beat up all five, and this gains him some respect. When Paul and Neil begin to meet other gay couples, it becomes clear to them that they have a new range of options to consider once they leave school. At the end of the book, at college, they are 'committed to making it as a couple'. Even Paul's father, who of all the family members had the most problems with the relationship, has come round to accepting it – to the point where he describes Neil as his son in law. This is a somewhat superficial book, close to the heterosexual teenage romance novel stereotype in some respects, but incorporating elements normally foreign to that stereotype (a physical as well as emotional relationship, the problems of prejudice to be overcome, and the explicit long-term commitment).

NEWMAN, Leslea

Heather Has Two Mommies
Alyson, Boston (1989)
ISBN 1-55583-180-X

This picture book, illustrated by Diana Souza, is intended for young children. Three-year-old Heather, the daughter of a lesbian couple, sees nothing unusual in having 'two mommies', until she joins a playgroup where the other children have 'daddies'. An explanation from a friendly adult at the playgroup and a session in which other children describe their different families help dispel her confusion. Despite the fact that it is intended for a young audience, this is a self-consciously 'issues-oriented' book (were it written for teenagers it would doubtless be described as a problem novel), in which such topics as artificial insemination, the birthing process, and the needs of a lesbian household have a place.

NEWMAN, Leslea

Gloria Goes to Gay Pride
Alyson, Boston (1991)
ISBN 1-55583-185-0

I llustrated by Russell Crocker, this picture book is aimed at children from three to seven years of age. Gloria lives with Mama Grace and Mama Rose. They celebrate holidays and special events together and one of these is Gay Pride. With their friends they march in the parade, carrying banners they have made. Gloria marches alongside Grace, Rose, their friend Richard and Richard's small son Jonathon. Along the way, people smile and wave at the marchers, but there is one group beside the road whose members 'aren't singing or clapping' and who have a sign saying 'Gays Go Away'. This becomes an excuse for a comment on attitudes to homosexuality, and Rose tells Gloria that 'some women love women, some men love men, and some women and men love each other. That's why we march in the parade – so everyone can have a choice.' But, over all, the Gay Pride Day is a 'fun day' for them all, with music, balloons, icecream cones, and games in the park.

NICHOLLS, Bron

Mullaway

Penguin, Harmondsworth (1986)
ISBN 0-14-008440-1

When Mum collapses on Christmas Day, the responsibility for holding the family together falls automatically to 16-year-old Mully. For the next year until her mother's death, Mully nurtures the family, sometimes bitterly resenting her enforced motherhood yet also realising her strength and capability in the role. Mully faces her brother Steve's experimenting with heroin use and his homosexual relationship with her secret love Guido, as well as neurotic behaviour from her brilliant younger brother Alan and her father's inability to communicate except through notes. Mully gains comfort from her friendship with her former English teacher, also a homosexual and one of her secret crushes. He persuades her to keep a diary, extracts from which form part of the novel. Perhaps overlong, this is nevertheless an honest, often funny, and thoroughly satisfying story of an ordinary Australian family.

NOONAN, Michael

McKenzie's Boots
(U.Q.P. Young Adult Fiction),
University of Queensland Press, Brisbane (1987)
ISBN 0-7022-2070-1

McKENZIE'S BOOTS
Michael Noonan

Rod Murray is the quintessential decent Australian who puts his age up to join the army at 15 and dies as a decorated hero at 17 in the mud of the New Guinea highlands. A secondary character who nevertheless plays an important role in the plot is a homosexual school teacher of Rod's whom he later encounters in New Guinea. There is an unspoken pact between them that Rod will keep quiet about Hillyard's past in return for the teacher's silence on his true age. Hillyard is finally killed in a suicidal act of bravery at a time when he is reportedly facing a charge of misconduct with a gunner. Rod is a character who is not inclined to censure, and although Hillyard is painted as an unattractive person, this is not particularly because of his homosexuality.

OLDHAM, June

Double Take
Viking Kestrel, New York (1988)
ISBN 0-670-82088-1

After Olivia Quinn plays the role of the landlady of a missing girl for a television docu-drama, she embarks on a private crusade to unravel the mystery of the girl's (and her landlady's) real-life disappearance. Her search seems to take her into a curiously homophobic world. She is attacked and abused in a pub one night because she is there with a gay man. A female friend describes an incident when she offered a lift to a woman waiting at a bus stop in the rain and was refused because the woman was frightened and thought she was trying to pick her up. As Olivia investigates the missing women, it seems at first that the landlady may have been running a brothel, then that they were lesbians. She finally discovers that they have been running an informal refuge for abused women. Homosexuality, whilst not the central concern of the novel, is a recurring motif. Oldham's elliptical and discursive dialogue, her offhand revelation of significant plot elements, and the intellectual and philosophical games the characters play make this at best a challenging read, and at times an obscure one.

OWEN, Gareth

The Man with Eyes Like Windows
Collins, London (1987)
ISBN 0-00-184547-0

L ouie's dad is a drifter and a dreamer, never settling to regular work, always trying to hit the show business big time. All Louie wants is for his father to come home and stay, and for his mother to want him there. In a rather picaresque novel, Louie sets out to find his father and persuade him to come home, learning a lot about himself, his father, and life as he goes. After leaving home, he hitches a ride with a man who, it soon becomes obvious, has sexual designs on him. He is an unpleasant character and threatens violence if Louie won't co-operate, but Louie escapes through the sun roof while they are stopped at a service station (the handle has been removed from the inside of his door). Although it is a fairly frightening incident for Louie, it is not referred to again and appears to be regarded as yet another in a series of adventures, and a lucky escape. This is an upbeat British novel, realistic and bittersweet in flavour.

PARK, Christine

Joining the Grown-Ups
Heinemann, New York (1986)
ISBN 0-434-57721-9

The grown-ups seem to know a lot of things that Josie at 17 longs to know – why her mother abandoned her husband and children to live with another woman, the quality of that relationship, and what her mother is like now. Josie journeys from Canada to England to see her mother, only to find Sylvia unhappy, preoccupied, and seemingly uninterested in her. In unravelling the grown-ups' secrets, Josie unwittingly releases them from stalemates they have been caught in and crosses into adulthood herself. Sylvia's lesbian relationship fascinates Josie but although it is discussed at length by various characters it is always at a distance and with little reference to its physical aspect. At times tedious, this novel does bridge the gap between adolescent novels and works of authors such as Iris Murdoch and Margaret Drabble.

PAUSACKER, Jenny

What Are Ya?

Angus and Robertson, Sydney (1987)
ISBN 0-207-15366-3
A new edition of this book was published in
the United Kingdom in 1991 by The Women's
Press under the title *Get a Life*
(Livewire Books for Teenagers)

Australian feminist and gay activist Jenny Pausacker was awarded an Angus and Robertson Writers Fellowship for this book. In it, she traces the changing ideas, feelings, and relationships of a group of young people in their final year at a city high school, as each, in his or her own way, attempts to adjust to the adult world. After a disastrous first time in bed with an insensitive boy, Barb wonders if she is a lesbian, until she discovers Paul and develops a steady relationship with him. Her friend Leith, wondering the same thing after a series of hopeless crushes, has an intense affair with another girl in her class. At first isolated and depressed because of her classmates' taunts about 'lesos', she becomes more secure in her feelings when she joins a club for young lesbians. While Pausacker's realistic dialogue is a strength of the book, a year is covered so rapidly, and so many people are introduced, that the reader cannot become deeply involved with the characters or fully understand their problems.

READING, J P

Bouquets for Brimbal

Harper and Row, New York (1980)
ISBN 0-06-024843-2

Bouquets for Brimbal describes two parallel teenage relationships, one heterosexual and one lesbian. Annie Brimbal and Macy Bacon, long-time best friends, have planned for many years to spend the summer vacation after their high school graduation working together at a summer stock theatre. Macy, who is heterosexual, works in the props department, while Annie is an aspiring actor who has already recognised that she is attracted to women. During the summer Macy becomes involved with Don, an actor in the company, while Annie begins an affair with Lola, an actor/director. While eager to share her feelings about her relationship with Don, Macy is reluctant to acknowledge her friend's friendship with Lola until she is directly confronted with its reality. The novel does present lesbian relationships in a positive light to heterosexual readers; however readers are still given a deeper insight into Macy's relationship with Don than into Annie's relationship. Since the book is written from Macy's perspective this is probably inevitable, and it does reflect the views of society as whole about heterosexual and homosexual relationships. Despite all this, the major theme of the novel is the importance of friendships and the need to resolve conflict and jealousy if a friendship is to be preserved.

REES, David

Quintin's Man
Dennis Dobson, New York (1976)
ISBN 0-234-77433-9

gainst all odds, precocious, clever Luke, son of a council worker, wins the love of Cheryl, conservative daughter of a local landowner. A self-assured boy who is loathe to admit any uncertainties in his world view, Luke is shocked to find that the older brother of a friend he has known all his life is gay, and to encounter a gay couple at one of his parties. The incident is quite lengthy but is irrelevant to the advancement of the plot or the development of characters, and seems designed to give the author an opportunity to display alternative lifestyles and expound a doctrine of tolerance. Luke is aggressively heterosexual in his relationship with Cheryl, and whilst he accepts Jack and his friends he pities those whom women cannot stir. A sequel to this novel, *The Estuary*, does find Luke taking a male lover.

REES, David

In the Tent
Dennis Dobson, London (1979)
ISBN 0-234-72091-3

T im, aged 17 and in his final year at an English secondary school, is beset by a number of problems, chief of which are his increasing awareness of his homosexual inclinations and his difficulty in reconciling this with the teachings of the Roman Catholic church in which he has been brought up. Inspired by his A-level history studies, he retreats into a fantasy world, imagining that he is in Exeter at the time of the civil war siege. A walking holiday in the Lake District with three classmates, which goes disastrously wrong when they are trapped by bad weather, forces him to begin an inner journey of self-discovery. Although Tim is seduced by classmate Ray, and has an affair with him, this is presented only through allusions and conversation – there is none of the explicit description of sexual activities such as is found in *The Milkman's on His Way*. The concern in *In the Tent* is much more with the inner conflicts of Tim (his own civil war) and the pressures on him.

REES, David

The Lighthouse
Dennis Dobson, New York (1980)
ISBN 0-234-72212-6

L eslie and Ewan, from *The Milkman's on His Way*, go to Greece together on holiday. They go their separate ways when Ewan meets a young Greek boy Christos and has an affair with him. Meanwhile, on Mykonos, Leslie meets Victoria, a young English girl holidaying in Greece before going to university. Their blossoming love affair, and its end when both return to England, is the real subject of this book. Ewan's meeting with Christos is only a passing incident in the story.

REES, David

The Milkman's on His Way

Gay Men's Press, London (1982)
ISBN 0-907040-12-8

Much more explicit than his other young adult books, this novel is about a young man growing up gay in modern Britain. While still at secondary school Ewan discovers that he is homosexual, and though he fancies his macho friend Leslie, the latter is interested only in girls. When his conservative parents find his diary, they are shocked by his 'tendencies', and Ewan leaves for London. There he plunges into a life of shallow relationships, gay bars, one-night stands, and promiscuity, until he meets and settles down into a monogamous relationship with James, a black student at London University. While the physical aspects of Ewan's various relationships are described in some detail, there is less emphasis on emotions. The point of view is almost that of a voyeur, rather than of someone deeply involved with the characters.

REES, David

The Estuary
Gay Men's Press, London (1983)
ISBN 0-907040-20-9

This novel forms a sequel to one of Rees' earlier books, *Quintin's Man*, and also incorporates characters from *In the Tent*. Luke, now a university graduate and employed in his first job as a newspaper reporter, has a year-long affair with the older and more sophisticated John. Cheryl, his former girlfriend, marries Aaron, the pop singer from *In the Tent*; they have a daughter, then split up when Aaron moves to California. Other gay couples and individuals have parts in the story, including Ray and Tim from *In the Tent* – still friends but no longer lovers. The book traces the changing patterns of the relationships of a group of people with ties going back many years. Not as well structured as *In the Tent*, or as explicit as *The Milkman's on His Way*, it fails to hold the interest of the reader, and seems to fade away rather than end satisfactorily. It is listed by the publishers as a 'novel for young people', but it is hard to imagine that it would hold the interest of teenagers.

REES, David

Out of the Winter Gardens

Olive Press (1984)
ISBN 0-946889-031-1

Mike doesn't know why his parents broke up when he was three or why he has had no contact with his father Peter in the 13 intervening years. When he is 16 his father invites him to stay, and Mike rather hesitantly sets off to spend two weeks with him. That Peter is gay stuns Mike at first, but doesn't unduly shock him or prevent him from wanting to get to know his father. Despite difficult scenes when Peter's lover Adrian moves out, Peter and Mike find they enjoy each other's company and Mike appreciates the open way he can discuss life, sex and sexuality with Peter. Although written from Mike's viewpoint, it seems likely that the book draws on the personal experience of the author as a homosexual parent. Mike is a likable young man and Peter is shown as a charming, complex man whose presence enriches Mike's life. The writing is gentle and even lyrical. This is an understated, reassuring story, even if perhaps a little optimistic.

REES, David

The Colour of His Hair

Third House, Exeter (1989)
ISBN 1-870188-10-1

As with some of David Rees' other novels, this one is difficult to define in terms of readership; however it does seem to be intended as much for young people in their late teenage years as for adults. It begins with Donald and Mark becoming lovers during their final year of secondary school in the mid 1970s, and their early stages of their affair occupy the first half of the book. The second half is devoted to the protracted breakup of their relationship 10 years later. While there are some fairly explicit descriptions of homosexual sex, along the lines of *The Milkman's on His Way*, there is much more discussion of the feelings and emotions of the main characters. In addition, the realities of the late 1980s intrude, with the introduction of AIDS and condoms. David Rees has announced that this will be his last novel.

RINALDI, Ann

The Good Side of My Heart

Holiday House, New York (1987)
ISBN 0-8234-0648-2

Teenager Brianna McQuade falls for her older brother's very attractive friend Josh, then Josh comes out as a homosexual and Brianna's world is all but shattered. A copy of this book has not been sighted but it is listed in several bibliographies, including that of Christine Jenkins (in which it has a long annotation).

RINALDO, C L

Dark Dreams
Gollancz, London (1975)
ISBN 0-575-01953-0

A review in the January 1986 issue of *Reading Time* (p40) identifies this as a book for young teenagers which deals with 'controversial themes', including 'accusations of homosexuality'.

A copy of this work has not been sighted.

SAKERS, Don

Act Well Your Part
Alyson, Boston (1986)
ISBN 0-932870-79-1

When 16-year-old Keith moves to a new town for his last two years of high school, he is lonely and unhappy at first and misses the company of his friend Frank. Then he joins the school drama club, where he meets the good-looking Bran Davenport and his group of friends. Keith and Bran fall in love, sleep together, and are recognised among their friends as a couple. Keith's mother is happy about their sexual relationship, while at school the senior students are very accepting and supportive of the boys who cuddle and dance together at parties and kiss each other in the canteen and in classroom doorways. The author makes the point, through Bran, that since this kind of behaviour is an acceptable part of boy/girl relationships in the school, it should be acceptable for two boys to behave in this way. The only real opposition to the relationship comes from one particular girl who is jealous because she feels that Keith has taken Bran from her. She persuades some of the other seniors to split with the two boys, but in an emotional scene at the school dance, which Bran and Keith attend as partners, these conflicts are resolved. A well-meaning but improbable book.

SAKERS, Don

Lucky in Love
Alyson, Boston (1987)
ISBN 1-55583-112-5

The main character in this novel is Frank, the friend who was left behind when Keith of *Act Well Your Part* moved to a new town. Frank falls in love with Purnell Johnson, black, handsome, athletic, intelligent, and star of the school basketball team. They meet at basketball practice, study together, and soon sleep together. They make no secret of their relationship. Not surprisingly, the romance is plagued by problems. Purnell says, 'Everybody's upset with us – my parents, your parents, the fellows, the cheerleaders ...' However, after various tribulations antagonistic classmates are more accepting, parents come round, and problems are ironed out as true feelings triumph. Purnell heads for college in another city; Frank, with another year of school to finish, finds the future wide open 'for him to make whatever he wanted of it. Maybe it would involve Purnell ... maybe some guy he'd not even met yet'.

SAMUELS, Gertrude

Run, Shelley, Run!
Crowel, New York (1974)
ISBN 0-690-00295-5

Described as a 'documentary novel for young adults', this book grew out of Gertrude Samuel's work as a reporter covering the juvenile courts throughout the United States. At the beginning of the book 16-year-old Shelley escapes for the third time from a Juvenile Centre for delinquent girls, this one in upstate New York. Her story to that point is told in flashbacks – a story of deprivation and abuse, of a child at the mercy of the adults around her, and of a system which is supposedly designed to protect her. When Shelley tells her mother that her stepfather has been 'touching' her, her mother refuses to believe her and hands Shelley over to state custody as 'unmanageable'. Shelley finds life in the centres difficult. The dreary atmosphere and the constant supervision are hard enough to cope with, but she has also to deal with the sometimes violent and case-hardened girls with whom she is living, and from whom she learns much about drugs, petty crime and sex. Some of the girls are on pot, some are retarded or in need of psychiatric help, and some are aggressive lesbians. Yet she cannot live at home with an alcoholic mother and a stepfather who molests her, nor can she legally live alone. The older lesbian girls at the Juvenile

Centre, like 'Mac' and the other big 'butches', are feared by Shelley and the younger girls, who are by and large powerless to resist their advances. Shelley says, 'Mac's very strong. No way I can keep her off me.' At each centre the scene is the same, with the younger girls at the mercy of the older and stronger ones. Committed for the third time and afraid of what the big girls could do to a loner like herself, Shelley allows Big Julie to make love to her regularly, and thus buys protection from the others. Later, a case worker who hears Shelley's story comments that it is the same in the juvenile centres for boys. While Shelley is eventually rescued and rehabilitated through the attention of a judge who is concerned at the conditions in the juvenile centres, others do not fare so well. The book at times reads like a case history notebook; nevertheless it does draw attention to a real social problem. Whether or not this is one that can best be addressed through a 'novel' for teenagers is another question.

SCOPPETTONE, Sandra

Trying Hard To Hear You
Harper and Row, New York (1974)
ISBN 0-06-025274-2

Perhaps this could more accurately be called trying hard *not* to hear you, which is what the narrator, 16-year-old Camilla, doggedly does over the summer that her best friend Jeff and her new boyfriend Phil fall in love with each other. The three are members of a youth theatre group which is putting on a musical. The violently negative reaction of the whole group to the two boys when the illicit love affair is discovered is quite shocking. In retrospect Camilla bitterly regrets her failure to support her friends; however she feels betrayed and disgusted by them. The summer ends tragically – Phil and one of the girls die in a car crash and friendships and alliances are torn apart – but in a postcript roll call it seems that the survivors have grown in tolerance and understanding. This is a classic 1970s problem novel and a rather dated read in 1991.

SCOPPETTONE, Sandra

Happy Endings Are All Alike
Dell, New York (1978)
ISBN 0-440-93376-5

Towards the end of their final year of high school, Jaret and Peggy fall in love. Both are bright, attractive teenagers headed for college, and they realise that in their small American town they will do well to avoid broadcasting their affair. However, people inevitably find out and they come under considerable pressure from some of their family and friends. But they really feel the force of community disapproval when Jaret is brutally raped by a young friend of her brother. He appeals for lenient treatment on the grounds that he went 'crazy' after seeing Jaret and Peggy making love in the woods. The book is fairly candid and realistic in its descriptions of the physical aspects of their affair, but less convincing in presenting their emotional involvement.

SEVERANCE, Jane

When Megan Went Away

Lollipop Power, Chapel Hill, North Carolina (1979)
ISBN 0-914996-22-3

Although it is not stated in this picture book that Shannon's mother is a lesbian, adult readers will assume that Shannon's mother and Megan are gay parents because of the living arrangements and because the book is dedicated to 'all children of lesbian mothers'. This has, in fact, been promoted as 'a divorce book' for children of lesbian mothers. Megan, who has been a kind of parent to Shannon as well as a friend to her mother, leaves the household and both Shannon and her mother are upset and unhappy, though both ultimately find comfort in each other. The illustrations are rather crudely drawn, but the detail in them may appeal to the intended audience of children aged three to six or seven years old.

SINGER, Marilyn

The Course of True Love Never Did Run Smooth

Harper and Row, New York (1983)
ISBN 0-06-025753-9

There are various 'true loves' which follow their course amidst the preparation for a high school play in this American novel for teenagers. None of them is smooth. Sixteen-year-old Becky becomes infatuated with Blake, a handsome new student. Her friend Nemi is attracted to Blake's sister Leila but by the time the show actually opens, the friendship between Becky and Nemi has turned to love. Meanwhile, the relationships of some of the secondary characters are also traced, including that of two of the other students, Richie and Craig, who fall in love. Thus the book describes a developing lesbian relationship between two main characters and a developing gay relationship between two of the secondary characters, as well as some heterosexual relationships. All are presented in a believable way.

SNYDER, Anne and PELLETIER, Louis

The Truth about Alex

New American Library, New York (1987)
ISBN 0-451-14996-3
First published 1981, as *Counterplay*

The truth about Alex is that he's gay. Brad, his best friend for two years, knows but no-one else does. Both boys are football heroes but when they are 17 and Alex's homosexuality becomes town gossip, not even football can protect him from vilification and persecution. His friendship with Brad supports him until Brad too becomes the target of innuendo and is ordered by his father and his coach to drop Alex as a friend. For Alex, his homosexuality is an unhappy and unwelcome condition and the resolution of the book is the boys' reconciliation as friends rather than Alex's acceptance of himself. This is an attractive, readable paperback which definitely falls into the 'problem novel' genre.

SOBOL, Rose

Woman Chief

Dial, New York (1976)
ISBN 0-4409-9657-0

Barbara Grier, in her 1981 bibliography, *The Lesbian in Literature* (third edition), lists *Woman Chief* as a title in which lesbian characters or incidents have a place. A copy of the book has not been sighted.

SPENCE, Eleanor

A Candle for Saint Antony
Oxford University Press, Oxford (1977)
ISBN 0-10-271415-5

When Justin first meets Rudi, a new boy at his Sydney high school, he despises him because his European background makes him 'different', but he quickly learns to appreciate those differences and becomes very friendly with Rudi. It is a friendship more intense than any other he has known. On a school trip to Vienna with the German class, he becomes aware that the other boys regard this friendship with some suspicion – comments about 'fairies' in the woods and such like are enough to alert him to what is going on. One evening in the Vienna Woods Rudi declares his love, but is overheard by one of the other boys. Justin, unable to face their scorn, breaks with Rudi, an action he will later regret. This is one of the very few Australian teenage novels to deal with homosexual feelings; it does so in a sensitive and non-judgmental way.

St GEORGE, Judith

Call Me Margo

GP Putnam's Sons, New York (1980)
ISBN 0-399-20790-2

Haywood is a very liberal girls' boarding school, but it is still a fertile breeding ground for bitchiness and rumours. Margo is 15 and new at the school and finds it difficult to make friends. Fortunately, she is a tennis star and the easy friendship and company of Miss Frye the coach partly compensates for the campaign of victimisation she is subjected to by her malevolent, crippled English teacher, Miss Durrett. At Miss Frye's tennis club Margo meets Pete, also a strong player, and is puzzled by Miss Frye's reluctance to let them play together. Eventually Margo stumbles on the dreadful truth: Miss Frye is a lesbian and she and Miss Durrett used to live together. Margo realises that everyone thinks there is more than simple friendship between her and her teacher and she is devastated. In a hasty happy ending, Margo accepts Miss Frye as a friend and is transferred from Miss Durrett's class; she and Pete start going out together and she makes some friends. Miss Durrett and Miss Frye are both rather desperate, pathetic characters and Margo is thin and unconvincing.

STONES, Rosemary (editor)

Someday My Prince Won't Come:
More stories for young feminists
Piccadilly Press, London (1988)
ISBN 1-85340-021-1

S even short stories comprise this collection. One, 'On the
Verge' by Susannah Bowyer, deals with lesbianism.
Seventeen-year-old Anna wonders if she might be a
lesbian, and speculates on just what it is that lesbians
'do'. It is her friend Carol who actually makes contact with a
young women's group in nearby Bristol and draws Anna into their
world. Common to the stories in this collection is a totally self-
centred, immature, mid-teenage view of the world, and also a
complete absence of sensible, mature adult characters. This makes
for depressing reading.

STORR, Catherine

Two's Company
Patrick Hardy Books, London (1984)
ISBN 0-7444-0039-2

Kathy and Claire, English teenagers on a family holiday in France, meet up by chance with two English university students, Steve and Val, and begin to date them. After some happy outings it gradually becomes clear that none of the relationships is really satisfactory, including that of Val and Steve. Kathy comes to realise that the boys have a homosexual relationship, though Claire, who is in love with Steve, refuses to acknowledge it. While there are no descriptions of sexual activities in the book, Val and Kathy do discuss homosexuality, and he tries to get her to realise that while he is interested only in boys, it is possible for some gay men, like Steve, to be interested in girls as well. The book is fairly insubstantial, and the problems of the various characters are presented in a superficial way.

STURGIS, Margaret

Danny
Alyson, Boston (1984)

Tom York teaches English at an American suburban high school. He is gay, separated from his wife, and dealing with the situation by immersing himself in his teaching job. Danny, one of his best students, becomes first a friend and then a lover, despite Tom's reluctance. As the story of an older man seduced by an aggressive teenager, it is not really successful: the characters are not sufficiently developed to make the scenario believable. Meanwhile, members of the Moral Majority have taken control of the school board and are campaigning to bring 'traditional values' back to education. Tom and Danny are found out, Tom is fired and Danny suspended. The book ends with Tom leaving town to find another job. The book is somewhat superficial, with contrived situations and little description or character development; no-one in the story really engages the sympathy of the reader.

SULLIVAN, Mary W

What's this about Pete?
Thomas Nelson, Nashville (1976)
ISBN 0-8407-6496-0

Pete is physically small for his age and has been a subject of scorn for some of his more macho classmates and teachers. His darkest secret is the fine handiwork he does to help his mother finish elaborate wedding gowns, for he fears that if any of his friends found out he would be branded a 'faggot' by them. In what is a plea for tolerance, Pete 'comes out' about his sewing, talks to a school counsellor about his fears that he is homosexual, and is finally content to let his sexual preference become clear in the future. The book is heavily reliant on stereotypes and has the feeling of being a set piece, purposely written, but it is fairly open and non-judgmental in its message, especially for its time.

TAX, Meredith

Families
Atlantic-Brown, Boston (1981)
ISBN 0-316-83240-5

F*amilies*, illustrated by Marylin Hafner, is a picture book for young children. It has appeared in several lists of children's books which depict a homosexual lifestyle. Beginning with Angie, who lives with her mother and visits her father, stepmother, and half-brother in another city, the book goes on to describe the families of Angie's friends. One child, Susie, 'lives with her mother and godmother', and this seems to be the basis for the book's listing as one depicting a homosexual family. However, as reviewer Virginia L Wolf has commented, there is nothing in the book that proves that the women are lesbians, 'although clearly their living arrangements raise the possibility' ('The Gay Family in Literature for Young People', *Children's Literature in Education*, volume 20, number 1, 1989, p 53).

TCHUDI, Stephen

The Burg-o-rama Man
Angus and Robertson, Sydney (1986)
ISBN 0-207-15319-1

A mid-western high school is chosen to feature in a series of commercials for the Burg-o-rama fast food chain as a typical American school in a typical American town. As a result of this decision, students learn about the power of money to corrupt, about junk food and about friendship. The search for stars for the commercials is the thread which connects episodes in the school life, seen through the eyes of Karen Wexler, editor of the school paper and commentator on events. One of these episodes is the branding of the talented male star of the school musical a 'twinkletoes'. Karen tries hard to convince his tormentors otherwise by showing how strong and macho he has to be to do the necessary lifts and strenuous routines, thereby proving that he couldn't be gay!

TOLAN, Stephanie S

The Last of Eden
Frederick Warne New York (1980)
ISBN 0-7232-6177-6

Mike (Michelle) has had an unhappy home life so it is her contented life at Turnbull Hall, her exclusive girls' boarding school, which nourishes her. As she enters her senior year her best friend is Marty, wealthy, aloof and artistic, and the year becomes a happy one as Marty paints and Mike writes. The serpent of sex enters this Eden however, and Marty is accused of a lesbian relationship with Louise, her painting teacher, while Louise's husband has an affair with a 15-year-old schoolgirl. The couple leaves and passions and jealousies subside until Marty enters into an all-consuming friendship with new girl Sylva and Mike is left, shattered, to contemplate her own sexuality and to try to rebuild her life without Marty. The reader is quite unengaged by these wooden characters; their sexual discoveries are as irrelevant and over-the-top as their triumphs and unhappinesses. Sylva incidentally tries to commit suicide.

TORCHIA, Joseph

The Kryptonite Kid

Holt, Rinehart and Winston, New York (1979)
ISBN 0-03-046676-8

The Gay Interest Group of the Canadian Library Association lists this as 'a disturbingly funny novel based upon an alienated boy's letters to Superman. The boy is gay without knowing it yet.' Jerry is certainly alienated, at home in a violent family and at school cowed by hellfire-breathing nuns. His only solace is his best (and only) friend Robert and their mutual devotion to Superman, whom they find it difficult to distinguish from the nun's omniscient, omnipotent God. Jerry's passion for Superman, his belief that he too can be super, and his slender connection with reality lead him to jump from a tall building, killing his father who tries to save him, and leaving him a quadriplegic. As his obsession with Superman intensifies, so does his passion for Robert. He dreams one night of going to a bar as an adult, searching for Robert, and finding the bar full of men, 'all looking for Robert. Their own Robert.' This is an uneasy novel, full of ambiguity. Jerry is portrayed as a very young boy preparing for his first Communion, totally ignorant of terms like 'petting', and unaware of what is meant when fellow students label him 'a queer' because he loves Superman. Jerry's innocent voice has, towards the end of the novel, to bear the author's more knowing perception of the world. The result leaves some confusion as to the novel's readership and appeal.

URE, Jean

You Win Some, You Lose Some

Bodley Head, New York (1984)
ISBN 0-370-30996-0

Jamie, hero of *A Proper Little Nooryeff*, decides to leave school and try to make ballet his career. To attend ballet school he must leave home, and his newly found independence makes it possible for him to pursue seriously his other ambition in life – sexual experience. He and flat-mate Steven discuss tactics and results as Jamie unsuccessfully works his way through the girls in their class. Smooth-talking Steven, however, has *his* eye on Jamie and tries to seduce him in a fairly good-natured scene, using classic seduction lines employed by either sex. A surprised Jamie resists and still manages to keep the friendship intact. The book closes with Jamie successfully moving in on his long-time friend Anita. Throughout the book slighting references are made to homosexuals in terms such as 'bum bandits' and 'poufdahs'; all the relationships are depicted in physical rather than emotional terms.

URE, Jean

The Other Side of the Fence

Bodley Head, New York (1986)
ISBN 0-370-30714-3

In a cross between *Good-night, Prof, Love* and *The Turbulent Term of Tyke Tiler*, the author tries to breach boundaries of class and sexuality. Well-to-do young university student Richard has a blazing row with his formidable father when he reveals that he has moved in with Jan, hitherto highly approved as a suitable 'friend'. Richard drives off wildly into the night and picks up Bonny, a tough, streetwise 16-year-old abandoned by her exploitative boyfriend. Their friendship enriches them both but Bonny's romantic illusions are shattered when, at the end of the novel, she discovers Jan is male. The reader has also been deliberately misled with derogatory comments about 'queers', 'poufs', and 'dykes' littering the way and never a pronoun used to refer to Jan. Although the book's obvious intent in its ending is to challenge and upset the reader's preconceptions and prejudices, the contrary may have already happened. A fairly self-conscious, British adolescent novel.

URE, Jean

The Trouble with Vanessa
Corgi, Reading (1988)
ISBN 0-552-52428-X

T his first volume in Jean Ure's trilogy based on life amongst the art and drama students in a London sixth-form college introduces Kate, Danny, Vanessa, Ned and others in their group. It is relevant to the theme of this bibiliography only in that two of the teachers are given nicknames with homosexual connotations: Miss Dando, 'a rather muscular woman', is 'Dykie Dando' and Mr Gordon is 'Gay Gordon'. Although Josh's possible homosexuality is an issue in the second volume in the trilogy, Josh is a very minor character in this first volume and no mention is made of his sexuality; in fact there is no discussion of homosexuality at all at this stage.

URE, Jean

There's always Danny
Corgi Freeway, London (1989)
ISBN 0-552-52429-8

The second book in a trilogy about life among the arts and drama students at a London sixth-form college, this follows *The Trouble with Vanessa*. Josh goes to live with Alan, an architect in his mid-30s, and Vanessa, Kate, Ned, Danny and the other students speculate about whether or not Josh and Alan are lovers. Even when it becomes known that Alan has AIDS, the exact nature of the relationship between Alan and Josh remains unclear. Apart from this, there are several discussions of AIDS and homosexuality between the students themselves, and between Kate and her very suburban mother. The points of view are varied – from Ned's and Danny's 'camp' take-off of 'Gay Gordon' the movement teacher at the school, to Kate's concerned attempts to understand Alan's perspective. However the book is not characterised by any great depth of feeling, though the realistic teenage dialogue is a strength.

WALKER, Kate

Peter
Omnibus, Norwood (1991)
ISBN 1-86291-065-0

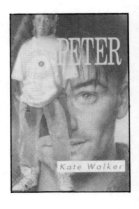

Peter is 15, into dirt bikes and curious about sex. His bike riding brings him into contact with a rather crude and cruel group of boys, and his best friend Tony is obsessed with having sex. When Peter meets David, a university friend of his older brother Vince, he is drawn to him, and when Vince tells him David is gay, Peter is terrified he may be also. Over several weeks of the summer vacation Peter has to assert himself in the bike group, withstand quite unsubstantiated taunts that he is gay, endure his father's violent reaction to graffiti labelling him as gay, and try to come to terms with his own sexuality. He is not aroused by a forthright advance from a girl Tony is pursuing, and tries unsuccessfully to seduce David, who reassures him that his sexual uncertainty is quite normal. By the end of the novel he is content to muck about with bikes for a while and leave sex until he is a bit older. He is also prepared to accept his sexuality, whatever it may be. This is a frank adolescent slice of life, with few literary pretensions but an accurate ear for contemporary Australian youth mores and manners.

WERBSA, Barbara

Run Softly, Go Fast
Atheneum/Bantam, New York (1970)
ISBN 0-553-11239-2

New York teenager David Marks, a sensitive artist, hates his materialistic businessman father. When his father dies of cancer, David, resentful, hurt, and bitter attempts to analyse the complex, intense, and antagonistic relationship they had. One particular scene makes the book relevant to the subject of this bibliography. In his last years of high school, David becomes close friends with Rick, whom his father considers to be a homosexual. Finding David and Rick wrestling one afternoon, his father loses his temper, calls Rick a 'queen', and throws him out. This is the cause of David's leaving home at 17 to live his own life as an artist in Greenwich Village. Although the incident is slight, it has a profound impact on David and on his relationship with his father. This is an intense, densely written, and introspective book which makes considerable demands on the reader.

WERSBA, Barbara

Tunes for a Small Harmonica
Pan Horizons, London (1976)
ISBN 0-330-29252-8

J F McAllister has trouble accepting her appropriate gender role. She chain smokes, dresses like a boy, and at nearly 17 is a sexual and emotional innocent with no interest in the opposite sex. She hypothesises that she must by gay, but exchanging a passionate kiss with her best friend Marylou and marching in a gay lib parade don't strike a responsive chord in her, so she concludes she is androgynous. When she and her analyst discuss why, contrary to appearances, she isn't gay, he offers her a glib explanation for homosexuality which she quickly demolishes. This is only a minor theme in a very funny, quirky book, but J F's calm acceptance of herself, no matter what that self may be, is a refreshingly healthy and uncomplicated attitude for an adolescent novel.

WERSBA, Barbara

Crazy Vanilla
Bodley Head, New York (1987)
ISBN 0-370-31056-X

Tyler is a loner. Once there had always been his beloved older brother Cameron as a friend and buffer against the world, but when Tyler was 12 the family discovered Cameron was gay and life and their relationship was never the same again. Tyler finds Cameron's homosexuality beyond him, as does his father. During the summer that he is 14, Tyler meets Mitzi, a tough, independent 15-year-old who shares his passion for nature photography and shows Tyler how to meet life head on instead of running away. Their love story is tender and innocent and the warmth of their relationship allows Tyler to reach out to his family, especially Cameron, again. Despite being very American, this is a delightful novel, touching universal adolescent concerns and emotions.

WERSBA, Barbara

Just Be Gorgeous
Bodley Head, London (1990)
ISBN 0-370-31296-1

Barbara Wersba

New York teenager Heidi Rosenbloom finds it very difficult to live up to the expectations of her divorced parents – her mother wants her to be beautiful and her father wants her to be brilliant. Unsure of her own identity and ill at ease with her appearance, she cuts her long hair and takes to wearing a huge, second-hand overcoat. Her fashionable mother takes this transformation as a personal affront, and their relationship deteriorates. Meanwhile, Heidi sees Jeffrey Collins tap-dancing outside a Broadway theatre and, to her mother's horror, befriends him. Their friendship is not without problems, since Jeffrey is gay and Heidi takes some time to realise that they can never be more than friends. However, their friendship is still a positive one: Jeffrey's optimism and love of life challenge Heidi to 'be herself'. Jeffrey's homosexuality is not really an issue in this book; rather, the focus is on Heidi and the influence that this friendship has on her.

WHEATLEY, Nadia

The Blooding
Viking Kestrel, New York (1987)
ISBN-0-670-82029-6

This is a complex novel about conflict: a large public conflict between timber workers and conservationists on the south coast of New South Wales; an internal conflict within the hero Colum, torn between his loyalty to the town and his father and his love for the forest; and the tensions which inevitably accompany a child growing up and away from his family. One of the intruders in the town is Garry from the office of the Minister for Conservation, whom Colum scathingly refers to as 'the poofter from the Ministry'. When Colum is in trouble, however, Garry proves both a friend and ally and at the end of the book Colum, with nowhere else to go, moves in with Garry and his lover Rick. Colum has also felt doubtful of his own sexual orientation, having dreamed one night about Garry, but is content to take Garry's word that he is straight. This is only a small element in a rich novel but is nevertheless significant in showing Colum's opening up to a wider, more diverse world.

WHEATLEY, Nadia (editor)

Landmarks
Turton & Chambers (1991)
ISBN 1-872148-65-4

This collection for young adults contains stories by nine prominent Australian authors. One, 'Off the Wall' by Jenny Pausaker, is particularly relevant to this bibliography. Its central character (unnamed) feels herself unconnected with her surroundings, both at home and at her alternative school. She is sustained by a constant internal monologue and finds relationships with her peers awkward, although she would like to enjoy them. One day she sees a new boy at the school and is immediately drawn to him. Her interest is noted by a group of girls who observe that it's not like her to show interest in a boy. Joel seeks her out after school and to her own amazement she confides in him that she is a lesbian. He tells her he knew she was and that he too is gay. She feels an overwhelming sense of fellowship and relief that she finally knows who she is and that she has an ally. A group of boys start to hassle Joel and she deals with them assertively but with humour. She and Joel are a team, and she understands that now she is free to create herself and her world as she wants them.

In another story, 'Only Two Hours by Train' by Bron Nicholls, two city boys go on a camping trip. The more adventurous of the two finds himself wondering about his friend's sexuality. 'Kevin found himself thinking back over the possibility of Theo being gay, and if so, would it make any difference to their friendship.' This is not explored further, but their friendship is strengthened by their shared experiences.

WILLHOITE, Michael

Daddy's Roommate
Alyson, Boston (1990)
ISBN 1-55583-178-8

Written for children aged two to five, particularly the children of gay men, this 32-page picture book describes the everyday life of a young boy who lives with his father and his father's lover, Frank. The book opens with the line 'My Mommy and Daddy got a divorce last year', and then, with a sentence and an illustration on each page, it shows Daddy and Frank living together, working together, and sleeping together in Daddy's house. During the weekends the two men and the young boy undertake activities common to all families – cleaning the house, cooking, shopping, relaxing, playing games, fighting and making up. As with Michael Willhoite's picture book *Families*, the treatment of homosexuality is straightforward and matter-of-fact. The book is attractive and well produced; the hard cover and full-page colour illustrations make it stand out amongst the generally cheaply produced picture books from the gay and feminist publishing houses.

WILLHOITE, Michael

Families:
A coloring book
Alyson, Boston (1991)
ISBN 1-55583-192-3

amilies is a colouring book for very young children. Each page has a large line drawing with a small amount of text (sometimes a couple of words, sometimes a simple sentence). The drawings show different families working together, playing together, visiting, looking after their pets. There are large families, small families, single-parent families, grandparents, uncles and aunts, adopted children as part of families, and so on. At least five pages are relevant to the theme of this bibliography. Tony Forelli's mother has moved in with 'a partner' after her divorce; one of the illustrations, captioned 'Now Tony has two Moms', shows Tony and the two women working in the kitchen. On the next page, the caption says 'Lisa Sinclair has two Dads, too', amd the illustration shows Lisa at the dinner table with the two men, while on the following page she is shown, again with the two men, meeting her 'new brother – sort of' at the airport. An illustration showing two women in a double bed, playing with two toddlers while drinking a morning cup of tea, is captioned 'Dwight and Dwayne were adopted by Clea and Beth'. The presentation of this material is simple, straightforward and matter-of-fact. There are no attempts at explanations, and no additional comments. If the fact that the pictures of gay and lesbian families show everyone looking happy could be interpreted as social comment (and it has been), then it also has to be said that all the other family groups (including a cat and her kittens) look happy too!

WILLMOTT, Frank

Suffer Dogs
Fontana Lions, Melbourne (1985)
ISBN 0-00-672355-1

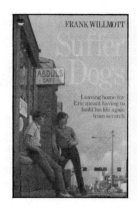

A gritty story of inner-city life and the kids who survive or go under. Two friends, John and Eric, are the central characters. Eric is a young, diffident newcomer fostered out to live with his aunt, and John a streetwise local. At the end of the novel, Eric has grown and matured into a sensitive, likeable adolescent but John has got his 'moll' of a girlfriend pregnant and is set for disastrous early marriage. The author constantly exposes these two characters to others who represent wider life options. One is a very sympathetically portrayed homosexual classmate who leaves school when the boys in the class turn on him; another is an adored male teacher about whom there are rumours of homosexuality. The gay characters fare much better than females in depth and sympathy of portrayal.

WILLMOTT, Frank

Here Comes the Night
Fontana Lions, London (1986)
ISBN 0-00-672453-1

This complex, many-layered Australian novel is included in this bibliography as an example of a book in which terms such as 'poofta' are used and references made to the possible homosexual inclinations of a particular character. There is, however, no evidence of homosexual behaviour.

Appendices
•
References
•
Index

I: Stories with homosexual main characters

Note: These lists do not include titles which have not been sighted. Some titles, such as *The Kryptonite Kid*, and *Your Family, My Family*, simply do not lend themselves to classification. Books are classified only where classification is easily made. Books appear alphabetically by title.

Act Well Your Part (Sakers)
All-American Boys (Mosca)
Annie on My Mind (Garden)
Bouquets for Brimbal (Reading)
The Boys on the Rock (Fox)
A Candle for Saint Antony (Spence)
Cody (Hale)
Crush (Futcher)
The Colour of His Hair (Rees)
The Course of True Love Never Did Run Smooth (Singer)
Dance on My Grave (Chambers)
Danny (Sturgis)
The Estuary (Rees)
Flick (Kesselman)
Happy Endings Are All Alike (Scoppettone)
Hey, Dollface (Hautzig)
I'll Get There. It Better Be Worth the Trip (Donovan)
In the Tent (Rees)
Independence Day (Ecker)
Just Hold On (Bunn)
Kiss: File JC 110 (Hoy)
Landmarks (Wheatley)
Lucky in Love (Sakers)
The Man without a Face (Holland)
The Milkman's on His Way (Rees)
The Other Side of the Fence (Ure)
Peter (Walker)
Reflections of a Rock Lobster (Fricke)
Ruby (Guy)
Run, Shelley, Run (Samuels)
Tunes for a Small Harmonica (Wersba)
What Are Ya? (Pausacker)
Who Lies Inside (Ireland)

II: Stories with homosexual supporting characters

Asha's Mums (Elwin & Paulse)
Breaking Up (Klein)
Brown Cow (Branfield)
Call Me Margo (St George)
Come out Smiling (Levy)
Crazy Vanilla (Wersba)
Different Friends (Jones)
Gloria Goes to Gay Pride (Newman)
Happily Ever After (Coleman)
Heather Has Two Mommies (Newman)
The Honesty Tree (McCauley)
A House Like a Lotus (L'Engle)
I'll Love You When You're More Like Me (Kerr)
Jenny Lives with Eric and Martin (Bosche)
Joining the Grown-Ups (Park)
Just Be Gorgeous (Wersba)
The Last of Eden (Tolan)
McKenzie's Boots (Noonan)
Mullaway (Nicholls)
My Life as a Body (Klein)
Night Kites (Kerr)
Now That I Know (Klein)
Out of the Winter Gardens (Rees)
Rebecca (Francis)
Sticks and Stones (Hall)
Thin Ice (Branfield)
Tinker's Career (Leonard)
The Truth about Alex (Snyder & Pelletier)
Trying Hard To Hear You (Scoppettone)
Two Weeks with the Queen (Gleitzman)
Two's Company (Storr)
Weetzie Bat (Block)
What Happened to Mr Forster? (Bargar)
You Win Some, You Lose Some (Ure)

III: Stories with homosexual background characters

Big Man and the Burn-Out (Bess)
Big Trouble (Limb)
The Blooding (Wheatley)
The Burg-o-rama Man (Tchudi)
The Chinese Garden (Manning)
Double Take (Oldham)
Elliott and Win (Meyer)
Family Secrets (Klein)
The First Time (Foster)
Go Ask Alice (Anon)
His Own Where (Jordan)
The Huaco of the Golden God (Logan)
Is That You, Miss Blue? (Kerr)
The Lighthouse (Rees)
Learning How To Fall (Klein)
Mac (Maclean)
The Man with Eyes Like Windows (Owen)
Me and My Mates (Macfarlane & McPherson)
Midnight Hour Encores (Brooks)
A Nice Fire and Some Moonpennies (Heffron)
Quintin's Man (Rees)
Run Softly, Go Fast (Wersba)
Suffer Dogs (Willmott)
Taking Sides (Klein)
There's always Danny (Ure)
What's this about Pete? (Sullivan)

IV: Stories which mention homosexuality or use homosexual terms

French Letters: The life and loves of Miss Maxine Harrison, Form 4A (Fairweather)
Goodbye Tomorrow (Miklowitz)
Here Comes the Night (Willmott)
I Never Asked You To Understand Me (DeClements)
Nobody's Family Is Going To Change (Fitzhugh)
Push Me, Pull Me (Chick)
Square Pegs (Hilton)
Tom Brown's School-Days (Hughes)
The Trouble with Vanessa (Ure)
Year King (Farmer)

V: Proportion of male to female homosexual characters

	Males	Females
Main characters	26	13
Supporting characters	21	10
Background characters	18	10
Total	65	33

VI: Characters by sex of author

(**Note:** it is not always possible to tell the sex of the authors by their names. Included in this table are the children's picture books omitted from Appendix V.

	Male Characters	Female Characters
Male authors	30	1
Female authors	34	31
Total	64	32

VII: Chronological list of titles

1954
The Diary of Anne Frank (Frank)

1962
The Chinese Garden (Manning)

1969
I'll Get There. It Better Be Worth the Trip (Donovan)

1970
Run Softly, Go Fast (Wersba)

1971
Go Ask Alice (Anon)
His Own Where (Jordan)
A Nice Fire and Some Moonpennies (Heffron)

1972
The Man without a Face (Holland)
Sticks and Stones (Hall)

1974
Run, Shelley, Run! (Samuels)
Taking Sides (Klein)
Trying Hard To Hear You (Scoppettone)

1975
Is That You, Miss Blue? (Kerr)

1976
Nobody's Family Is Going To Change (Fitzhugh)
Quintin's Man (Rees)
Tunes for a Small Harmonica (Wersba)
What's this about Pete? (Sullivan)

1977
A Candle for Saint Antony (Spence)
I'll Love You When You're More Like Me (Kerr)
Year King (Farmer)

1978
Happy Endings Are All Alike (Scoppettone)
Hey, Dollface (Hautzig)
I Am Maria (Hellberg)

1979
In the Tent (Rees)
The Kryptonite Kid (Torchia)
Ruby (Guy)
When Megan Went Away (Severance)

1980
Bouquets for Brimbal (Reading)
Breaking Up (Klein)
Call Me Margo (St George)
The Last of Eden (Tolan)
The Lighthouse (Rees)
Your Family, My Family (Drescher)

1981
Crush (Futcher)
Come out Smiling (Levy)
Families (Tax)
The Truth about Alex (Snyder & Pelletier, originally titled *Counterplay*)
Reflections of a Rock Lobster (Fricke)
What Happened to Mr Forster? (Bargar)
The Wing and the Flame (Hanlon)

Chronological list of titles

1982
Annie on My Mind (Garden)
Dance on My Grave (Chambers)
Just Hold On (Bunn)
The Milkman's on His Way (Rees)

1983
All-American Boys (Mosca)
Brown Cow (Branfield)
The Course of True Love Never Did Run Smooth (Singer)
The Estuary (Rees)
Flick (Kesselman)
Independence Day (Ecker)
Jenny Lives with Eric and Martin (Bosche)
Thin Ice (Branfield)

1984
Danny (Sturgis)
The Boy in the Off-White Hat (Hall)
A House Like a Lotus (L'Engle)
Out of the Winter Gardens (Rees)
Two's Company (Storr)
Who Lies Inside (Ireland)
You Win Some, You Lose Some (Ure)

1985
Big Man and the Burn-Out (Bess)
The Boys on the Rock (Fox)
Family Secrets (Klein)
The Honesty Tree (McCauley)
Suffer Dogs (Willmott)

1986
Act Well Your Part (Sakers)
The Burg-o-rama Man (Tchudi)
Elliott and Win (Meyer)
Happily Ever After (Coleman)
Here Comes the Night (Willmott)
I Never Asked You To Understand Me (De Clements)
Joining the Grown-Ups (Park)
Midnight Hour Encores (Brooks)
Mullaway (Nicholls)
Night Kites (Kerr)
The Other Side of the Fence (Ure)

1987
The Blooding (Wheatley)
Cody (Hale)
Crazy Vanilla (Wersba)
Different Friends (Jones)
French Letters (Fairweather)
Goodbye Tomorrow (Miklowitz)
McKenzie's Boots (Noonan)
Mac (Maclean)
The Man with Eyes Like Windows (Owen)
Lucky in Love (Sakers)
My Life as a Body (Klein)
Push Me, Pull Me (Chick)
What Are Ya? (Pausacker)

1988
Double Take (Oldham)
The First Time (Foster)
The Huaco of the Golden God (Logan)

The Journey (Marsden)
Kiss File JC 110 (Hoy)
Now That I Know (Klein)
Someday My Prince Won't Come (Stones)
Tinker's Career (Leonard)
The Trouble with Vanessa (Ure)

1989
The Colour of His Hair (Rees)
First Loves (Malone)
Heather Has Two Mommies (Newman)
Learning How To Fall (Klein)
There's always Danny (Ure)
Two Weeks with the Queen (Gleitzman)

1990
Asha's Mums (Elwin & Paulse)
Big Trouble (Limb)
Daddy's Roommate (Willhoite)
Just Be Gorgeous (Wersba)
Weetzie Bat (Block)

1991
Bonjour Mr Satie (dePaola)
Families: A coloring book (Willhoite)
Gloria Goes to Gay Pride (Newman)
How Would You Feel if Your Dad Was Gay? (Heron & Maran)
Landmarks (Wheatley)
Me and My Mates (Macfarlane & McPherson)
Peter (Walker)
Rebecca (Francis)
Square Pegs (Hilton)

1954	1	1980	6
		1981	7
1962	1	1982	4
1969	1	1983	8
		1984	7
1970	1	1985	5
1971	3	1986	11
1972	2	1987	14
1973	0	1988	9
1974	3	1989	6
1975	1	(1980-89)	77
1976	4		
1977	3	1990	5
1978	3	1991	9
1979	4		
(1970-79)	24		

References

— 'Homophobia and Education', *Interracial Books for Children Bulletin*, vol. 14, no. 3 and 4 (special issue) *passim*

ALLEN, Jane et al (compilers), 1989, *Out on the Shelves: Lesbian books into libraries*, AAL Publishing, London

AUBREY, Sean, 1973, 'Queer Reading', *Librarians for Social Change*, 4, Winter, 17

AUCHMUTY, Rosemary, 1987, 'You're a Dyke, Angela!', *Trouble and Strife*, 10, Spring, pp 23-30

AUCHMUTY, Rosemary, 1989, 'You're a Dyke, Angela!: Elsie J Oxenham and the rise and fall of the schoolgirl story' in *Not a Passing Phase: Reclaiming lesbians in history 1840-1985*, The Women's Press, London, pp 119-140 (This is a longer version of the above article published in 1987 in *Trouble and Strife*.)

BESS, Clayton, 1988, 'In Protest', *Voya*, February, pp 274-275

BRITTAIN, Vera Mary, 1968, *Radclyffe Hall : A case study of obscenity*, Femina, London

CADOGAN, Mary and CRAIG, Patricia, 1976, *You're a Brick, Angela!: A new look at girls' fiction from 1839-1975*, Gollancz, London

Canadian Library Association Gay Interest Group, 1982, *Out on the Shelves: Gay and lesbian fiction list: A selection guide*, Canadian Library Association, np

CHEATHAM, Bertha M, 1986, 'The Year in Review', *School Library Journal*, December, pp 23-29

CLARK, Margaret, 1988, 'Publishing for Teenagers', *Books for Keeps*, 49, March, pp 10-11

COCKSHUT, A O J, 1977, *Man and Woman: A study of love and the novel, 1740-1920*, Collins, London

References

DAMON, Gene, WATSON, Jan, and JORDAN, Robin, 1975, *The Lesbian in Literature: A bibliography*, (2nd edn), The Ladder, Reno, Nevada

FORREST, Lyn and COX, Merrillee (compilers), 1989, 'Lesbian Content in Books for Children and Young Adults', *Lesbian Network*, 21, September, pp 34-35

FOSTER, Jeannette H, 1985, *Sex Variant Women in Literature*, (3rd edn, with addenda by Barbara Grier), Naiad, Tallahassee, Florida

FRANK, Josette, 1973, 'Sexuality in Books for Children', *Library Journal*, 15 February, pp 621-623

FREEMAN, Gillian, 1976, *The Schoolgirl Ethic: The life and work of Angela Brazil*, Allen Lane, London

GOODMAN, Jan, 1983, 'Out of the Closet, but Paying the Price: Lesbian and gay characters in children's literature', *Interracial Books for Children Bulletin*, 14, 3/4, pp 13-15

GRIER, Barbara, 1981, *The Lesbian in Literature*, (3rd edn), Naiad, Tallahassee, Florida

HANCKEL, Frances and CUNNINGHAM, John, 1976, 'Can Young Gays Find Happiness in YA books', *Wilson Library Bulletin*, 50, 7, March, pp 528-534

HOLLAND, Isabelle, 1973, 'Tilting at Taboos', *The Horn Book Magazine*, 49, 3, June, pp 299-305

JENKINS, C A and MORRIS, Julie L, 1983, 'Recommended Books on Gay/Lesbian Themes', *Interracial Books for Children Bulletin*, 14, 3/4, pp 16-19

JENKINS, Christine, 1988, 'Heartthrobs and Heartbreaks, a guide to young adult books with gay themes', *Out-look*, Fall, pp 82-92

References

KUDA, Marie J, 1974, *Women Loving Women: A bibliography*, Lavender Press, Chicago

RIDDELL, Gordon R, 1989, 'Bibliography of Lesbian Writing' (review), *Library Association Record*, 91, 8, August, pp 488-489

SAPHIRA, Miriam, 1988, *New Lesbian Literature 1980-88*, Papers Incorporated, Auckland

SMITH, Linda, 1986, 'Breakfast in Bed's a Gay Affair', *Sunday Times*, 21 September, p 41

TAYLOR, Anne, 1988, 'What Shall We Tell the Children?: Changing social attitudes as reflected in literature for young readers', *Emergency Librarian*, January/February, pp 9-15

THORNE, Alison, 1988, 'Lesbians in Literature', *Freedom Socialist Bulletin*, 3, 1, Summer, pp 18-23

WARNER, Philip, 1976, *The Best of British Pluck: The boy's own paper*, Macdonald and Jane's, London

WERSBA, Barbara, 1973, 'Sexuality in Books for Children', *Library Journal*, 15 February, pp 620-623

YOUNG, Ian, 1982, *The Male Homosexual in Literature: A bibliography*, (2nd edn), Scarecrow, Metuchen, New Jersey

Title Index

Act Well Your Part	Sakers, Don
All-American Boys	Mosca, Frank
Annie on My Mind	Garden, Nancy
The Arizona Kid	Koertge, Ron
Asha's Mums	Elwin, Rosamund and Paulse, Michele
Big Man and the Burn-Out	Bess, Clayton
Big Trouble	Limb, Sue
The Blooding	Wheatley, Nadia
Bonjour Mr Satie	dePaola, Tomie
Bouquets for Brimbal	Reading, J P
The Boy in the Off-White Hat	Hall, Lynn
The Boys on the Rock	Fox, John
Breaking Up	Klein, Norma
Brown Cow	Branfield, John
The Burg-o-rama Man	Tchudi, Stephen
Call Me Margo	St George, Judith
A Candle for Saint Antony	Spence, Eleanor
The Chinese Garden	Manning, Rosemary
Cody	Hale, Keith
The Colour of His Hair	Rees, David
Come out Smiling	Levy, Elizabeth
The Course of True Love Never Did Run Smooth	Singer, Marilyn
Crazy Vanilla	Wersba, Barbara
Crush	Futcher, Jane
Daddy's Roommate	Willhoite, Michael
Dance on My Grave	Chambers, Aidan
Danny	Sturgis, Margaret
Dark Dreams	Rinaldo, C L
The Diary of Anne Frank	Frank, Anne
Different Friends	Jones, Rhodri
Double Take	Oldham, June
Elliott and Win	Meyer, Carolyn
The Estuary	Rees, David

Title Index

Title Index